Look! You're Dancing
A memoir of dogs, dance and devotion

Joyce A. Miller

Richmond, VA

Copyright © 2022 by **Joyce A. Miller**

All rights reserved. No part of this publication may be reproduced, distributed or transmitted in any form or by any means, without prior written permission.

Joyce A. Miller
www.joyceamiller.com

This work is a memoir. It reflects the author's present recollection of experiences over time. Some names and characteristics have been changed, some events have been compressed, and some dialogue has been recreated.

Book Layout © 2022 BookDesignTemplates.com
Book Cover © 2022 Oliver J. Dimalanta

Look! You're Dancing / Joyce A. Miller. -- 1st ed.
ISBN 978-1-7354963-2-0 Paperback
ISBN 978-1-7354963-3-7 E-book

Dedicated to all those who truly, madly, deeply love their dogs.

First Written Description of Any Breed:

A Greyhound should be headed like a snake
And necked like a drake,
Footed like a cat
Tail like a rat
Backed like a beam,
Sided like a bream

—1486 Dame Juliana Berners,
the Abbess of Sopwell Priory

CONTENTS

How It All Started 1
Go Away for a While 9
Greyhound Pets of America 19
Home Visits 25
Miz Betsy Rose 33
Canine Freestyle Federation 41
Easter on Parade 49
Motley Crew 57
Nursing Home Therapy Dogs 67
My Poor Girl 75
Things People Say to Greyhound Owners 85
A Greyhound Puppy? 87
James River Greyhounds 95
Hit the Road, Jack 101
Pet Crazy 109
Free Fallin' 115
Jefferson Lab 123
PG Arrives 133
Coax me 139
Beach Bound Hounds 147
Things Gifted To Me 155
A Little White Wedding Chapel 157
Grapehounds 165
Walking the dogs 173

Surprising Suffolk 181
Things That Go Bump in the Night 189
Long Goodbye 193
Epilogue 201

Chapter 1

How It All Started

This is a story about companionship, trust, and love—about how many times a woman gives her heart away to her dog.

It all started innocently enough. When my daughter Jade was seven years old, she was invited to a friend's birthday party at the Peninsula SPCA Petting Zoo. The Petting Zoo was a fenced-in enclosure with several picnic tables, a big red wooden barn, and a variety of barnyard animals for the children to feed and pet.

Cleverly, the shelter was set up so that one had to walk past the kennels of adoptable dogs to enter the barnyard area. We were a little early, so to use up some time, we looked at the puppies along the way.

Jade's long brown hair, tied up in a ponytail with a pink scrunchy, bobbed up and down as she skipped through the kennels. She suddenly stopped short in front of one newspaper-lined cage. In the back of the cage was one dark brown, furry puppy with one blue eye and one brown eye, slouched over on its side.

"Mom! Look at this puppy! Look at his eyes! Isn't he cute?" She knelt and, before I could stop her, stuck her fingers into the crate. The puppy was very friendly and licked her fingers instead of biting her.

"Yes, he's very cute," I replied absent-mindedly as I glanced through the doorway to see if the birthday party was finished setting up.

"Can I have him? Please, please, please, Mom?" Jade begged.

"We're here for a birthday party. Not to adopt a puppy," I said.

"Please, Mom?"

"Look, you go home and ask Mr. Al if you can have a puppy. If he says yes, then we'll come back and get the puppy," I told her while thinking to myself that Alan, my husband and Jade's stepfather, for sure would say no. My kids called their stepfather Mr. Al. It was something we picked up when we moved to the south where kids called adults Mr. or Mrs. along with their first name. It became a term of endearment.

Jade seemed to have forgotten about the puppy as she enjoyed feeding the goats and chickens with the other kids.

But when we got home, the first thing she did was run to her stepfather.

"How was the birthday party?" Alan asked her.

"Mr. Al, Mom said I can have a puppy if you say it's all right," she said immediately. He looked over her head to me expectantly for some explanation of what answer he was supposed to give her.

"She saw a cute puppy with one blue eye and one brown eye. I told her if you said it was all right, she could have the puppy."

"If you get up with your mother every day for a week and help her walk her dog, you can have the puppy," he said to Jade. We already had an older bull terrier named Dottie. I walked Dottie every day at 5:30 a.m. before I went to work.

"A week?" I said to him later when we were alone. "Dogs live for ten to fifteen years! Of course, she can do it for a week!"

And she did. She got up every day for a week and went on the walk with me in the early morning darkness just as the sun was coming up. She helped me put Dottie's kibble in her food bowl.

Jade was so excited when we returned to the shelter the following week to pick up her puppy. We searched through all the kennels, but the puppy with the unusual eyes had disappeared. She hung her head. I told her to look through the rest of the kennel. Maybe there was another puppy she would like to have.

"No," she said stubbornly. "That was the puppy I really wanted." I heaved a sigh of relief as we prepared to walk out the door. A lucky escape for me.

Someone from the staff saw us leaving and yelled out to us, "Have you two seen Daisy?"

I turned around and said, "Thanks, but I think we've seen every puppy in the kennels."

Undeterred, the kennel worker said, "Come with me," and guided us into a back room. I'm sure this puppy was the next in line to be euthanized. She introduced us to a small black puppy with white markings, maybe a combination of black lab and border collie--it was anyone's guess. I noticed her puffed-up belly full of worms connected to her crooked, little back legs. Her eyes were a little runny. The woman handed the puppy to my daughter.

Jade hugged Daisy to her chest. Daisy whimpered and snuggled up to her neck. Jade looked up at me with big blue eyes and said, "Mom, I love her."

While we were at the desk filling out the paperwork for the adoption, the kennel worker took me aside and whispered to me, "If there's something seriously wrong with her, you can bring her back." I knew what that meant.

Daisy went home with us. That afternoon I took her to the vet, and indeed she had many of the problems I envisioned. She was full of worms and had bad hips. The vet said, "If you wanted a puppy, why didn't you tell me? I could have gotten you a healthy puppy."

For about a month, Jade took care of Daisy. She got up, walked with me, and fed her. Then one day she said, "Daisy can be the family dog now, Mom. I don't want her to be just my dog anymore," which I translated to mean, "You can walk her and feed her, Mom."

Now I had Dottie and Daisy to walk together each morning before work. Dottie didn't have the same feelings of affection for Daisy as the rest of the family. Daisy hid from Dottie in the laundry room since Dottie growled and snapped at her at every encounter. We discovered that Dottie had some health issues specific to the bull terrier breed and we returned her to her breeder. The breeder agreed that it was in everyone's best interest if Dottie was returned.

Because Daisy was a rambunctious, energetic six-month-old puppy, I started taking her to classes at a local facility called Merrimac Dog Training Club. I took her through the basic training. She learned to sit, lie down, stay, and come when called. She graduated with the Canine Good Citizen (CGC) designation. The CGC program was designed by the American Kennel Club to bring a consistent set of basic behaviors to be taught and tested to ensure a dog was trained to a level of good companionship.

Despite her health problems, she became a splendid companion, and I enjoyed training her. She was the first dog I ever trained. But because she was a mixed breed dog, in the 1990s there weren't many opportunities for me to compete with her in any dog sports. To compete in Obedience or Agility with the American Kennel Club (AKC) she had to be a full-bred dog. (That has since changed, and many mixed breeds now compete in multiple sports that the AKC offers.)

I met a woman at the dog training club, Marilyn, one of the best dog trainers. She had strong problem-solving skills when it came to dogs. She could read the subtleties of dog and human body language and knew what the dog was going to do before anyone else. To me, she was the dog whisperer. She owned pugs and a Doberman but knew much about many other breeds. In her day job, she was a primary school reading specialist, and that must have been where she got her patience and resilience. Her hair was always dyed in some crazy color combination and cut in a quirky style, sometimes black on the underside and white on top. She bought her clothes at thrift shops and then adorned them with paintings or sewing to make them her own style. I immediately wanted to be friends with her.

One day at the dog club, she asked me to watch a video with her. It was called *Getting Started with Sandra Davis,*

Pepper and Jabba: Dancing with Your Dog. Jabba was a black giant schnauzer, and Pepper was a border collie. Sandra Davis was a petite woman with short black hair who trained her dogs to do freestyle moves in the dining room of her home. The instructional video showed how to perform twenty different freestyle moves.

"They call this canine freestyle or dog dancing," Marilyn said. "We can do this. This is something anyone can do because the dogs don't have to be purebred. The dog dancers have their own organizations like the Canine Freestyle Federation and the World Canine Freestyle Organization. It's very popular in the UK and Europe. You should try this with Daisy."

Marilyn explained further. "Compare it to pairs ice skating. You teach the dog to do a series of tricks and behaviors. You find a piece of music that matches the dog's gait. You choreograph the dog to do the behaviors along with the music, and it looks like you and the dog are dancing. If you compete, you get both a technical score for doing the behaviors properly and an artistic score for how well the dog and your costume fit the music. And there are different levels of competition that get progressively more challenging, requiring more advanced dog tricks and behaviors, and are longer in duration."

At the end of the video, Sandra Davis had videotaped two of her performances. The first was with Pepper to "Achy, Breaky Heart". Sandra wore a fringed, sequined western shirt and a cowboy hat. Pepper had a matching bandanna. I loved their line dance performance with lots of two-stepping. But the best part of her whole training video for me was that in most of the training exercises, she used the giant schnauzer,

Jabba. He was big and slow enough that I could follow the demonstrations. Jabba's final performance on the tape was to "New York, New York." He wore a bowtie, while Sandra had a white, blousy tunic, black bowtie, top hat, and black leggings.

So, I started training Daisy to dance with me. I was hooked. Over a few months, I taught her to spin, to circle me, to weave through my legs as I walked, to circle a cane as Sandra Davis demonstrated, and other fun skills. Once she knew some different behaviors, it was time to add some music. A song was picked to match the dog's gait. Daisy had a lilting gait due to her bad hips, but we picked a snappy instrumental song for her, "Swing Time," from an old Fred Astaire movie.

Because Marilyn was a primary school teacher, we had many opportunities to take the dogs to schools where we performed for children. I wore a tuxedo shirt with a black bow tie and black pants, and Daisy wore a white tuxedo collar with a red bow.

On the stage in front of the audience of rapt, up-turned little faces, I felt butterflies in my stomach. Daisy looked up at my outstretched hand, and my spirits brightened. I could barely conceal my delight when she did all the tricks in the right order, and we moved across the stage like soldiers doing the jitterbug before heading off to war. At the end, the kids crowded around to pet the dancing dogs. Daisy soaked up all the attention.

In addition to Daisy, I had also rescued a Walker hound mix named Willow. Because everyone I met at the dog training club had multiple dogs, I got caught up in the culture and thought I should have another dog too. Willow had severe hip dysplasia and kept her back feet together when she walked. Her gait was more of a step, step, hop, so Willow was not a candidate for dog dancing. I just enjoyed listening to her happy baying welcome when I returned home from work.

Dogs don't live as long as we would like, and probably due to her poor health at the beginning of her life, Daisy passed away at age six after a bout of pancreatitis. I kept her alive much longer than I should have. It was selfish of me, but I couldn't bear the thought of letting her go.

I truly loved the feeling of connection while performing with Daisy. I enjoyed the flow of our movement through the music and felt such joy, but when she was gone, I also felt so much grief.

I wanted to continue doing dog dancing. I thought about what kind of dog partner I would like to have. I'm a tall, plus-size woman, five feet ten inches tall and over 200 pounds, so I decided I wanted a big dog. But I wasn't sure what breed I wanted.

So, I had just lost Daisy, and I had really been bitten by the canine freestyle bug. I wanted a dog to train, and I had none. Sometimes it's best to step away from a problem to get some perspective. I went to France.

Chapter 2

Go Away for a While

Some people lose a dog and right away go out and get another puppy or another rescue. But that wasn't me. I had a different timetable for my grief. I needed to feel the deep sadness of losing my dance partner and accept that she was gone.

I worked at a nuclear physics laboratory called the Thomas Jefferson National Accelerator Facility in Newport News, Virginia, known as Jefferson Lab. If one has dogs, one has to work to pay for them. I still had Willow, and she required some health care.

At the lab, I did mechanical design work and designed the experiments for the visiting physicists. It was interesting, challenging work. An additional perk was that my husband Alan also worked there. In fact, he interviewed me for the role, but more on that later. One of the best things about working there was meeting the physicists who came from all over the world to conduct experiments. At the very beginning of my tenure there, we met some physicists who became lifelong friends.

In 2000, shortly after Daisy passed, one of these friends, Pascal from France, called and asked us if we wanted to accompany him to take his sailboat on a two-week-long trip down the Canal du Midi into the Mediterranean Sea.

Before I could accept, I had to find someone to take care of Willow. One of my friends, Jan, ran the education department at the lab. She loved dogs like I did and rescued rough collies. The rough collie is a herding breed, and the most well-known example of the breed is television's Lassie. I asked Jan if she would take care of Willow while I went to France, and she enthusiastically agreed. She may not have been so keen to keep her if she had smelled her oily coat beforehand.

The trip was on. The Canal du Midi is a 150-mile-long canal through southern France that connects the Atlantic Ocean to the Mediterranean Sea. Pascal and his brothers had built a twenty-six-foot sailboat named *La Gargouille*, The Gargoyle. Pascal had sailed *La Gargouille* around the United Kingdom and Ireland in the North Sea but wanted to move it to the Med. He planned to take the boat through the lock system of the canal. Some of his brothers took the boat through the hardest part of the canal over the Pyrenees Mountains. Pascal knew that he and Alan shared a love of fishing and boating, so he thought we would enjoy the trip.

Joining us was Helene, a physicist who had grown up in the same region where Pascal's family lived. Helene was half my size in stature but had twice the size of my heart. She was a true vegetarian and never wanted to harm a single living thing. I once saw her stop her car, get out and move a snail from one side of the road to the other so it wouldn't get smashed on the road. And Pascal's college-age niece, Anne-Priscille, came along too.

Pascal picked us up at the airport in Paris. After a breakfast of café au lait, served in a bowl rather than a cup, and croissants, we drove to a wonderful house in Riom where Pascal's mother lived. The house, which to me looked more like a castle than a house, had been in Pascal's family since the eighteenth century. It was built from a gray, local volcanic rock called volvic and topped with a red tile roof. The rooms were filled with antiques and oil paintings of Pascal's forefathers. After dinner, Anne-Priscille played the piano for us while Alan and Pascal played a game of billiards.

After a few days of rest to get over our jet lag, we got up and drove to Lissac, the village where Helene lived. We had lunch with her in the courtyard of her restored stone farmhouse. It was the first time we had been to her house, and I loved how quaint it was. She had no refrigerator but kept her perishable items in a cave under the house. I was falling in love with this provincial French culture I was being exposed to.

We took two cars and began the 275-mile drive south. Pascal and Helene had both packed their cars with supplies for the trip. We squeezed our two sleeping bags in with the boxes of non-perishable goods and bottles of water. We left Helene's car in the village of Beziers. Then, with all of us in Pascal's car, we made our way to the medieval village of Carcassonne where Pascal's brothers had left the boat in a marina for us. We arrived after midnight, quickly stowed our gear, and went to sleep on the boat.

The trip was beginning to feel like something out of a stereotypical French movie—our arrival in Paris, with the Eiffel Tower, Notre Dame, and the Arc de Triomphe, followed by a visit to Pascal's ancestral home filled with beautiful art and antiques. We were eating the best French cheeses and drinking French wine. The romantic perception of this country was helping me to get over losing my dog.

Before getting under way in the boat, we toured the walled city of Carcassone. Helene told us a folk story about the owner of the castle, Madame Carcas, coming under siege. Surrounded by the enemy, the people inside the castle were surely going to starve to death. Madame Carcas had them slaughter the remaining pigs and throw them over the wall. When the invading marauders saw that, they thought, "If these people have enough livestock to throw dead animals over the wall, we will never be able to wait them out." So they retreated. There was much joyous ringing of the bells when this happened. It may be where the term "carcass" originated.

After the tour of the walled city, we headed back to the marina and Gargouille. Taking the sailboat down the canal involved dismantling the twenty-five-foot-long mast so the boat would fit through the tunnels along the way, but Pascal's brothers had done that. When the water in the canal got shallow, we all had to sit on the gunwales of one side and lean our bodies over the edge of the boat to tilt the keel out of the water so we wouldn't get stuck. Each day we traveled—motoring, not sailing—as far as we wanted and stopped in some small French village.

The first village we stopped at was called Trebes. We walked into the village and bought food to prepare for dinner on the boat. It was here that I realized we hadn't brought any jackets or pullovers with us. Although it was September in the South of France, it still got chilly at night. We slept in the boat at night, and I was happy to crawl into my warm sleeping bag in the front cabin of the boat.

We bought fresh baguettes to dip into our café au lait in the morning. If we passed something interesting, Pascal would moor the boat. We stopped at a village called Marseillette just to have a beer in a café. We saw people taking wedding photos with the scenic canal as a backdrop.

The lockmaster at Puicheric sold bottles of wine to go with our dinner. He also made these fantastic sculptures from wood and grapevines. On one side of the lock were Adam and Eve. On the other side was a group of playful animals, an elephant overlooking the lock and an alligator at the exit. In the distance, I saw a sculpture of a woman walking a dog. I wasn't expecting it, and it made me pause and inhale quickly.

"It reminds me of Daisy," I said to Helene. With all the excitement of seeing new sights each day, I had forgotten about her for a while.

She rubbed my arm as she said, "You will start to feel better, and you will find another dog to love just like Daisy." I wanted to share her confidence.

We had a head (nautical language for a toilet) on the boat but no shower. One evening, we moored next to a closed miniature golf course. A faded sign with the words "*Le Chat Qui Pêche*" and a picture of a cat dancing with a fishing pole hung over the entrance. Anne-Priscille, Helene, and I took buckets from the boat, filled them with water at one of the golf course holes, stripped off our clothes, and showered some of the dirt rings off our necks. I could feel the dirt washing off me. Even my sunburn and scrapes felt better afterward.

We stopped along the way at an ancient archaeological site called Oppidum d'Ensérune. We climbed several miles to the top of this hill town, a Gallic settlement from Roman times between the sixth century BC and first century AD. There were huge terracotta vases, the size of a small room in a house, buried around the settlement, that at one time held grain. From the top of the hill, we had a panoramic view of the wedge-shaped fields below that radiated from a central depression. Pascal read from a plaque that said ditches along the edges of the fields allowed water to flow to the center where it was piped to other places in the south. They began doing this in the thirteenth century, and it is still functional today.

As we spent so much time exploring Oppidum, we reached the six-level lock at Beziers just as it was closing for the night, so we could not go through the locks. Helene rode the bike that was on the boat back to retrieve her car and then stayed with us one more night. I felt a small ache in my heart, and I cried when she left the next day. I was going to miss spending the days with her. We had a strong connection during the whole trip, and I knew I wasn't going to see her again for another few years. I felt sad about that. On top of that, Helene missed out on experiencing where the canal passed over the Orb River in an aqueduct called the Pont de Neuf—a canal going over a river.

We stopped at a small harbor and walked two kilometers to the Mediterranean Sea. I waded into the pristine blue water. Anne-Priscille and Pascal went swimming but it was a little too cold for me. I did pick up a smooth seashell and still carry it around in a pocket of my purse to remind me of that day.

At the end of the canal in the city of Sète, Pascal had the mast re-attached at a boatyard. In Sète, I was finally able to buy a couple of sweatshirts at a tourist gift shop for Alan and me. Anne-Priscille laughed when she saw the classic navy-blue-and-white-striped nautical sweatshirt I wore over top of my lilac dress. By that point, however, we were in a spot with warmer temperatures, and I didn't need the sweatshirt as much. We set sail for Toulon, the eventual mooring spot for La Gargouille.

After a day of sailing, where Pascal even let Alan man the rudder, we arrived at the port, Saint Maries de la Mer. It was a magical place with wild, white Camarque horses and pink flamingoes. Did I mention this was like living in a movie? The night before we arrived, there had been a bullfight in town. Although I didn't want to see a bullfight, we did eat some of the bull at a restaurant that night, served up as steaks for the patrons.

There was a yellow lab at the restaurant, who came and plopped down beside our table. His face was covered with so many mosquitoes that it was hard to tell what color it was. I felt so sorry for him but didn't want to brush those mosquitoes away. At the table, we talked about the old Aesop's Fable about the fox and hedgehog where the fox swims across the river and is covered by flies. A hedgehog comes along and offers to drive the blood-sucking flies away. The fox tells him to leave that swarm of flies because they are already full. If he drives them away, a new swarm will come and take what little blood he has left. The lab was such a docile, relaxed dog—I didn't want to subject him to a new swarm of mosquitoes. Maybe I should consider a sweet yellow lab as my next dance partner?

The trip from Saint Maries de la Mer to Marseille took about eleven hours. There was steady wind when we started out, around seven knots. But halfway into the day, the wind died, so we had to rely on the motor. When we reached Marseille, we found out they were having a sailing race, and there was hardly any space open in the marina. Finally, the *captainerie* told us we could stay near his office if we promised to be gone by 8:00 a.m. the next day.

We hiked up to a church, the Notre Dame de la Garde, at the top of the highest point of Marseille. There was a lower church built from rock in the Romanesque style and an upper church decorated with mosaics in a Byzantine style. Atop the bell tower was a huge copper statue of Madonna and child.

As we waited outside for Pascal to finish exploring the church, a woman with two harlequin Great Danes approached us. I tried to take Alan's picture with them, but one kept trying to jump up on his shoulders and put Alan's head into his mouth.

"*Ils sont inoffensifs*," the lady said. "They're harmless."

They were beautiful black and white dogs. As I was considering tall dogs for my dancing partners, these would have been tall enough for me. Maybe I should consider a Great Dane for my next dance cohort?

In Marseille, Alan and I caught the high-speed train back to Paris, and Pascal continued to Toulon. In Paris, Alan and I had one more day before we returned to the United States. We visited the Louvre but were so tired we could barely trudge through the galleries. I did look at paintings of dogs by their masters' sides. In the paintings, border collies and poodles were depicted as intelligent dogs. By the end of the trip, I hadn't made any decisions about a new dog, and I was too tired to think about it anymore.

When our plane touched down back in the United States and we returned to our everyday lives, I still hadn't decided on a breed for my next canine dancing partner. I didn't want to get a dog before we went on the long trip because that would have affected our initial bonding. I had seen several different dog breeds while on the trip, but none of them called to me. I considered a hunting breed like a vizsla or a German short-haired pointer because they would probably get along well with Willow and they were tall leggy dog breeds.

Someone left a Winter 2000 copy of *Celebrating Greyhounds* magazine at the dog club. I picked it up to read the main article, "Life with the Class Clown." All the silly attributes in the article, like standing out in a crowd and demanding attention, made it sound like a greyhound would make a great dancing partner. And ironically, the dog's name in the article was Dancer! The magazine also offered several articles on what was involved in adopting a greyhound. In the photos, I saw that they were tall, sleek, and would look good out on the dance floor. And there were so many of them available for adoption when their racing careers ended. Maybe I should consider a greyhound for my dancing partner?

Chapter 3

Greyhound Pets of America

I contacted a greyhound rescue group that I found on the internet called Greyt Expectations. On its website, I saw that there were eighteen recognized coat colors for greyhounds: black, white, brindle, fawn, red, or a combination of these colors. Oddly enough given the name of the breed, gray was a rare color for a greyhound. Right away I thought this was a great beginning for picking a dog. I could get whatever color I wanted. On the page with adoptable dogs, I saw a red fawn female with the most beautiful eyes outlined with kohl black eyeliner. Maybe my daughter and I were not so different falling for these dogs because they had beautiful eyes.

Immediately, I filled out the detailed, three-page online application. I listed Marilyn's name, my next-door neighbor, and my vet on the application as my references. The paperwork to adopt a child is probably more detailed than this was—but not much more. The group's president, Gil, called me after receiving the application, and I explained my plan and why I wanted a greyhound.

"This is going to sound crazy, but I want to do dog dancing with this greyhound," I explained. "You can think of it like pairs ice skating. You teach the dog to do a series of tricks like spins and weaving between your legs. You choreograph the dog's behaviors to a piece of music, and it looks like you and the dog are dancing."

"Uh-huh," he said, nonchalantly. "Cool." I wasn't sure if this meant I would get a greyhound or not.

"It's not like a circus act. The dog doesn't walk around on its hind legs and wear a tutu," I added nervously. I wanted him to understand that I was serious.

Gil laughed out loud, and I felt relieved. I guess he was picturing a greyhound in a tutu.

"I'm going to need you to read the following two books: *Retired Racing Greyhounds for Dummies* by Lee Livingood and *Adopting the Racing Greyhound* by Cynthia Branagan," Gil said when he regained his composure.

"I've been looking at your website and I'm interested in the red fawn female," I said.

"Well, I have already promised her to someone else, but there are plenty of other hounds in need of homes. I'm going to need to talk with your references, and I'll get back to you," Gil said.

A day or so later, my next-door neighbor told me she had been contacted. "Someone from a greyhound group called me and asked for a reference about you adopting a greyhound. When I was talking with him on the phone, I was looking out the window, and you were in the backyard throwing a frisbee for Willow. That's what I told him," my neighbor said, smiling over the fence.

It wasn't long after that Gil called and said he thought the track in Jacksonville, Florida had a hound that would work for me. She was a young, black-and-white tuxedo greyhound with the race name of A Bar Kit. He said Kit was very playful and would probably enjoy dog dancing. She had raced nineteen times and won four races. But she wasn't the best of the litter, and her owners put her in the adoption kennel. The adoption group was moving her from Jacksonville to Richmond, Virginia, and I could pick her up on the weekend.

It's my understanding that the kennel where Kit raced was named A Bar after the bar that holds the fuzzy lure the greyhounds chase during a race. The lure is usually a stuffed rabbit or a stuffed bone. Most of the dogs' names in this kennel went alphabetically and usually contained only three letters. There were seven puppies in Kit's litter, but only five ended up with race records—three females (A Bar Kay, A Bar Kel, and A Bar Kit) and two males (A Bar Max and A Bar Mik). Greyhounds have tattoos on their ears. Kit's left ear had 88550 and her right ear had 50G. The left ear is the litter registration number assigned by the National Greyhound Association. The right ear identifies the month, the year, and the order in the litter. So, Kit was born in May, designated by the five in the tattoo, the year 2000, designated by the zero, and she was number seven, designated by the seventh letter of the alphabet, G. She was the baby of the litter.

I drove to Richmond to meet this skin and bones dog with a dry, lackluster coat. She was skinnier than a normal greyhound, and her teeth were gray from some antibiotics the track personnel had given her as a young dog. Despite her appearance, she was vivacious and high-spirited. To me, Kit was Daisy in a greyhound suit. I took her home.

I decided to call A Bar Kit just Kit or Kitty. Who calls a dog Kitty? Although greyhounds are quiet, clean, and love to lounge around in a sunny spot—very catlike in their disposition—I probably gave her some identity issues. Here Kitty, Kitty!

Since I had trained Daisy, I knew what I had to do with Kit. I had learned to use a clicker with positive reinforcement training. A clicker is a small handheld plastic box with a metal piece inside. When the metal piece is pressed, it makes a sharp, short clicking sound. When used in dog training, the trainer clicks when the dog performs a specific behavior. The click tells the dog that he has done what you've asked him to do. The timing of the click is critical, and a reward follows every click. Usually, the reward is food, but it can be anything that the dog finds rewarding. I soon realized that greyhounds have only been trained to race. Mostly they stand up or they lie down—not much in between.

It took me several months to train Kit to sit. Marilyn devised a method that she thought would work. She had me cradle Kit's chest with one arm and hook the other arm around her backside until Kit lowered it. Then I would click and treat her as soon as her butt touched the floor. In the process, I found out that Kit would do almost anything for salmon treats. Drool would spill from her mouth when I pulled out the salmon. So I didn't give up, and soon she was sitting. That seemed to unlock the learning key, and, in a twinkle, she was able to circle me, spin, and sidestep. The sidestep was one of the more difficult dance moves, but her long legs made it a little easier. I got such a thrill whenever she learned something new!

As Kit grasped how to perform these behaviors, I realized I had to learn more about this breed and the racing world to understand how to train this dog to her full potential.

I got back in touch with Gil. He had dissolved his adoption group, Greyt Expectations, and joined forces with another greyhound adoption group, GPA, Greyhound Pets of America. GPA already had a few members in the Richmond area, and Gil explained that if he joined them, they could do more to help bring the greyhounds from the tracks in the south. The group became GPA-Richmond.

GPA-Richmond's mission statement was "to find responsible loving homes for greyhounds, to acquaint the public with the desirability of greyhounds as pets, and to promote greyhounds for adoption."

Many people who rescue greyhounds relate to this oft-repeated starfish parable. One day an old man was walking on a beach with thousands of starfish that had been stranded during high tide. He came upon a young boy who was throwing starfish back into the water one by one. He asked the boy what he was doing. The boy replied he was throwing the starfish back into the water because they couldn't make it back there by themselves. When the sun got high in the sky, the starfish on the beach would die unless he continued to throw them back. The old man said there were thousands of starfish on the beach and the boy really wouldn't be able to make much of a difference. The boy bent down, picked up another starfish, and threw it as far as he could into the ocean. He smiled at the man and said, "It made a difference to that one, and it made a difference to me."

As with any commercial enterprise that involves animals, one can always find horror stories. Greyhounds are not exempt. The authorities arrested a security guard from a track in Alabama when it was discovered that he would take unwanted hounds and shoot them for ten dollars each. They located a mass grave with over 3,000 bodies at his Alabama farm. He said he had been shooting the dogs no one wanted since he was sixteen years old. He was sixty-eight. The racing owners had the dogs killed because they were no longer profitable. In 2002 when I adopted Kit, records show that 20,000 greyhounds were euthanized nationwide.

I wanted to do what I could to get more greyhounds adopted into homes. Showing that greyhounds could do things other than racing, like dancing, might be helpful.

Chapter 4

Home Visits

I joined forces with Gil and the others to save as many greyhounds as we could. I lived in Hampton, Virginia, about ninety miles south of Richmond. I agreed to do home visits in the Tidewater/Hampton Roads area and to foster hounds so we could adopt out more dogs. Gil coordinated with kennel workers in Jacksonville to bring the hounds from Florida to Virginia. I would take Kit along with me to the home visits so the potential adopters could see exactly how big a greyhound would be in their homes. The home visits were about an hour long. My job was to check on whether the home was suitable and safe for a greyhound. I would assess the family members and any other pets in the home. Some greyhounds are cat and small dog safe; others have a higher prey drive and are not safe because they chase small moving objects by instinct.

One thing that greyhounds have trouble with is going up and down the stairs, especially wooden stairs that are open in the back like those found on decks. When they lived at the kennels at the track, they only ever had to walk on one level. At the kennel, the most they had to do was jump into a crate that had been stacked on the top of another crate or jump into the hauler truck. It seemed to freak them out to look through the openings in the back of the steps. The steps don't look solid enough to walk on if there is an opening in them.

One of my first home visits in Norfolk, Virginia was to a beach home that was right on the Atlantic Ocean. The house of gray weathered wood built on stilts over the sand had about sixty wooden deck steps leading up to the home's entrance. There was no elevator. As soon as I pulled up in front of the house and saw those steps, I knew no greyhound could live there. Kit balked at going up the steps. She would go up one or two and then jump back down into the sand.

I had to return Kit to the car and went to meet the prospective adopters. I was stiff and uncomfortable as I shook their hands and introduced myself.

"I'm sorry, but I don't think we can place a greyhound here. If you come outside with me, I can show you that my dog will not go up your steps."

We went outside. I got Kit out of the car. And again, she would go up one or two steps and jump back down.

The man said, "I'll carry the dog up and down the steps."

I crossed my arms over my chest and countered with, "You'll carry him for about two weeks and then you'll call me to come and get the dog. These dogs weigh about seventy-five to eighty pounds."

"But other dogs go up and down steps."

"That's true," I said. "And maybe you need to adopt another breed. All I can tell you is that a greyhound will not go up and down all those steps."

Both the man and his wife looked disappointed as I loaded Kit back into my car and drove away. I didn't want to turn them down but felt it was not a good home for a greyhound.

The home visits where I turned people down are more memorable to me than the ones where everything was fine. Each volunteer had a checklist of items to go over. It included asking if their landlord allowed large dogs; making sure there were no obvious holes in the fence that a hound could squeeze through; checking the gates to make sure they latched securely; asking the potential adopters to put stickers at hound eye height on sliding glass doors to avoid the hounds getting hurt. I also had to explain that their new dog had probably never seen a ceiling fan before and might freak out when it was turned on. Furthermore, greyhounds could have trouble walking on a hardwood floors and might need some additional rugs. But sometimes it wasn't these obvious things that would cause me to turn someone down. It would just be a feeling in the pit of my stomach.

One such visit I had in Williamsburg, Virginia. The home was a townhouse with no yard, so I had to explain to the single woman who lived there that she would have to leash walk the dog. When Kit and I entered her house, she had a gazelle or an antelope rug on the floor. I paused and took a step back. I thought that was an odd choice of decor for an animal lover. We sat on the sofa to talk, and Kit was giving me the eye like she wanted to jump up on the sofa with me. She wanted no part of lying on the dead gazelle on the floor.

Kit kept inching closer and closer to my knee and pushing her head onto my lap as we talked. "I think she wants to get up on the sofa," I said.

The prospective adopter's reaction was a side-eye that said, "Do NOT let her get up on my sofa!"

To defuse the situation, I asked her if we could walk around outside so she could show me where she planned to leash walk her dog. Greyhounds need to be kept on a leash because they are great hunters and will disappear in seconds if they see a small animal to chase. When we walked through the dining room, there was a bearskin rug, complete with a head sporting a full-on snarl, under the dining room table. Kit wanted no part of that! She didn't even want to walk by it! I coaxed her out the sliding glass door, and then we didn't go back into the house. I told the adoption group that maybe this wasn't the best home for a greyhound or any dog, and the woman never followed up on her adoption application.

There was another house visit in Suffolk, Virginia where we pulled up and parked our car. The house had several concrete steps leading up to the porch. Kit seemed to take that in stride, but just as the front door opened, there was a loud scream-like squawk from inside the house. Kit froze at the front door. She was not going inside. It made me pause, too, as I wondered myself if someone was getting beat up or worse, murdered.

It turned out that this family had a small private zoo. They had two noisy birds, four ferrets, and an older hound. It was one of the squawking birds who made the scream we had heard. I ended up giving them approval when I observed their interactions with Kit. They said Kit could go around to the back of the house and enter through the backyard, so she didn't have to walk past the noisy bird. They were very relaxed and patient and didn't rush her. I was a little concerned about the ferrets triggering a greyhound's prey drive, but I figured this family knew a bit about their animals and would introduce the greyhound slowly to the rest of their pack. I realized their expectations aligned with the reality of adopting a greyhound. If I had a rubber stamp that said "Approved," I would have slapped it in red ink onto their application.

As good as that home visit turned out, another one was quite shocking, and I will never forget it. I arrived at the house in Yorktown, Virginia on a Sunday afternoon as we had arranged. As I pulled up, I noticed a man was arriving by car at the same time. He looked at me a little strangely and followed me to the front door of the house. I rang the doorbell.

A woman came to the door, and she was crying. She held open the door for both of us to go inside, and I introduced myself.

"I'm Joyce, and I'm here from the greyhound adoption group. But maybe this is a bad time," I said.

"No, no, no. I've been waiting for you. This is Brother Donald," she said as she introduced me to the man who had walked up to the house with me.

"Where is he?" Brother Donald asked her.

"John!" she called upstairs. "Brother Donald is here for you."

A teenage boy came down the steps with his head hanging. He was crying.

"This seems like a really bad time," I said. "Maybe I should go."

"No, please stay," she begged. "John is going to leave with Brother Donald so they can talk." They went out the front door, and she escorted me into their family room. We sat down on the couch.

"You're probably wondering what is going on. This is not the first impression I had hoped to make," she said. "My husband is in the military, and he's gone on deployment much of the year. It's very difficult for John. That is one reason we wanted to get a greyhound. We thought the dog could be a companion for him while my husband is away. Today at church, some of the other kids were teasing John. They wouldn't let him join their group. When we got home from church, they continued to taunt him on social media. John climbed out of his bedroom window onto the roof of the house and threatened to jump off. He wanted to end his misery. That's when I called Brother Donald from the church and asked him to come and speak to him."

"I really think this is a bad time to be talking about getting a dog. It seems like you have more important things on your mind," I said.

"No, really. This is a help. If we could talk about the dog, it would take my mind off the other things," she said.

So, we went through the checklist and walked around their home. It was a great place for a greyhound, with carpet throughout the house and a 6-foot privacy fence around the backyard. She was a stay-at-home mom, so she would always be there for the dog.

After our home visit check, we went back to the family room and sat down again.

"I really think having a dog will help John. It will give him a sense of purpose, another living thing to take care of," she said.

"You're really putting a lot on this dog. They're the ones who need rescuing," I said.

I ended up approving them for their dog because I knew from my own childhood that having a pet to take care of could make all the difference. And it reinforced my decision to become a secular humanist. Secular humanists are concerned with human welfare and happiness and believe that this is the only world—there is no afterlife. Those church kids were so cruel! Bullying is such a big problem. I believe in the "Golden Rule" where you treat people the way you want to be treated. It didn't seem like they had learned that lesson.

I also appreciate the idea of a Rainbow Bridge that leads to a lush, green meadow where all the dogs you've had in your life are waiting for you when you die. The thought of reuniting is a heartwarming feeling, but I don't really believe it. I believe there is an energy that leaves their bodies and reunites with the earth's energy, and you can always feel them around you.

Any time I did a home visit, I had to answer the question, "What does it take to make a safe home for a greyhound?" The answer is a little patience and foresight about transitioning them from a racing regimen to a home life. They thrive around human beings and other greyhounds and dislike being alone. I weighed whether a dog would blossom in the home, and that's how I made my decision. So, as unsettling as that last home visit had been, I felt in my heart that a greyhound would thrive there.

Chapter 5

Miz Betsy Rose

One day Gil called and asked me if I would foster a brood mom, Miz Betsy Rose. This black greyhound mom was eleven years old. In the 1996-97 season, she ran 29.23 seconds at Palm Beach, the fastest time ever for a female there. She had several litters which produced twelve pups. Miz Betsy Rose's trainer had worked with her for her entire life. Then he had a falling out with her owners and got fired. When he was packing up his things to go, he went to the kennels to take Rosie with him, but the owners told him to leave her. They were putting her up for adoption.

So, I drove to Richmond to pick up this very frightened old girl. She had never lived in a house before and had never ridden in a car until that day when a caravan brought her to Richmond from Florida. When I looked at her closely, I noticed that half of her nose was missing, and she had a very stiff, coarse coat. Gil thought she probably had run into the fence at the end of the racetrack when she couldn't stop in time. Her bristly coat could have been a holdover from one of her distant relatives as some lurchers have wiry coats.

When we got back to our house in Hampton, she paced around and around until she finally settled uneasily on a pillow at the very end of our dark hallway. Even Kit couldn't calm her down. Rosie was a huge greyhound with a massive chest for a female. When we let her outside to run in the backyard, she could cross it in three strides.

After I had her for about a week, Gil called and told me someone wanted to come and look at her, possibly to adopt her. He said, "If this lady wants to take her home, there's no charge for adopting her. We don't even think she'll live another six months due to her age."

After work the next day, a woman showed up at my house in a conversion van with captain's chairs and side windows with blinds. She was stout and middle-aged with short brown hair. There was nothing really out of the ordinary about her, but, again, I had that feeling in the pit of my stomach that told me it wasn't right.

She burst into the house and said, "This dog is FAMOUS. She holds the track record as the fastest female. Everyone has heard of Miz Betsy Rose."

I had never heard of Rosie until the day I picked her up in Richmond. I tried to temper her enthusiasm. "Well, she's not so famous anymore. She just needs a soft place to lay her head in retirement."

The woman said she wanted her, but before she took her, she desperately wanted to take some pictures of her. We coaxed Rosie down the hallway, and we went outside into the backyard for picture taking. Rosie stood next to our grape arbor and the woman snapped away.

"People won't believe me. I have to get some pictures of her because she's FAMOUS," she said.

The woman talked some more as we watched Rosie and Kit run around in the backyard. She later revealed, "I have four greyhounds and a boxer at home. And sometimes I don't get up early enough in the morning, and one of them will have a little accident in the house. My husband and I are in the middle of a divorce."

I was thinking to myself, "This does not sound like an ideal retirement home for Rosie. How will she fit into this pack of dogs? It will be so difficult for her." Some people who rescue dogs begin to think they are the only ones who can care for the dogs. It's a short step from that idea to ego-driven hoarding situations. I had read many articles about the subject online.

Just then Alan arrived home from golfing. He came into the backyard and said, "Oh, so you're the woman who is taking Rosie?"

I stood facing Alan but behind the woman. I tried to signal to him by slashing my hand in front of my neck to show that I wanted him to stop talking. He stopped talking but had a confused look on his face.

Then she stopped taking pictures of Rosie, turned to me, and said, "Of course, you're the foster family, so I understand you get first dibs on adopting her."

Immediately, I jumped in. "Yes. You know, I'm sorry you had to come all this way to meet her, but we're going to keep her."

Alan shot me an odd look.

"Well, I'm just going to take a few more pictures of her, and then I'll go. No one will believe that I've met this FAMOUS dog. I can hardly believe it myself," she said.

The woman seemed just as happy to have taken Rosie's picture as she would have been if she had taken Rosie home with her.

As we watched her drive away, my husband asked, "What was that all about?"

"I guess we have two dogs now," I said and then explained my gut feeling.

I wasn't comfortable granting Rosie's adoption to this person. Greyhounds who are safe and secure in their surroundings sometimes sleep in a position called roaching. They lie on their backs and stick all four feet into the air like a dead cockroach. The position exposes their whole underside and is, therefore, a vulnerable posture. When Rosie finally roached at our house, I knew she felt at home.

I continued to train Kit for canine freestyle dance, and Rosie just lounged around the house. Rosie went on walks with us and built up her endurance. At first, she only walked around the block, but soon she was joining Kit and me at Sandy Bottom Nature Park in Hampton and walking for a mile on the trail around the lake. When we got to the part of the lake where the dogs could wade into the water if they wanted, Kit always jumped in while Rosie waited patiently on the trail.

Our walks were not always peaceful, though. On one walk through our neighborhood, we had a dreadful experience. I walked the dogs as soon as I got up at five-thirty or six in the morning before I went to work. It was usually still dark. One morning we walked past a house that had a vehicle parked partially in the driveway and blocking the sidewalk. Kit and Rosie walked ahead of me on 6-foot leashes. As they rounded the car's bumper, the leash jerked in my hand. Kit snatched a cat up from the sidewalk!

"Drop it! Drop it!" I yelled at Kit. I cringed as Kit shook the cat instead of dropping it.

The owner came running out of her house. By that time, I had gotten to Kit and managed to make her release the cat. Instantly, Rosie grabbed the cat from the street. By now the dogs had tangled the woman and me up in the leashes as we struggled to get the cat away from the dogs. The woman fell to the ground with the cat in her arms.

She screamed, "Just get away from me!" as I tried to help her get up. "Just get those dogs away from me."

"I'm going to take the dogs home, and then I'll come back to help you with your cat," I replied as I dragged Kit and Rosie toward my house.

"Just leave us alone," she said as she cried big tears. Her knees were bloody from falling on the pavement and the cat was moaning in her arms.

Within the hour I went back to her house, but no one was home. I was sure she was at the emergency vet.

I left a note on her door. It said, "I'm so sorry about what happened this morning with your cat. I love all animals, and this was a horrible accident. I will pay your vet bills, and I hope your cat is okay." I left my name and contact information.

She contacted me later that day. The cat had to be euthanized. I told her again how sorry I was and that I would pay the vet bill and for cremation if she wanted.

As we spoke, she told me through tears, "Our cat was named Misty. She was 22 years old. Every morning I would let her outside, and she would lay by the mailbox. When I went out to pick up the paper, I would carry her back inside. She was like a child to me."

My heart ached. I felt like she had put a knife in my heart and twisted it. I knew what it was like to love an animal that much. If I could have brought the cat back to life, I would have, but we all know that isn't possible. So I offered the only thing I could think of.

"If you find a kitten that you want anywhere, I will pay for its travel and adoption fee for you," I proposed. I knew a new kitten couldn't replace Misty, but I had to try.

She thanked me, but I never heard from her again.

This incident brought back a painful memory from my childhood. When I was about seven years old, I had a silver tabby cat named Francis. We lived in a rural area, and, as most cats did, she went in and out of the house throughout the day. She wasn't an indoor cat. Indoor animals were not the norm in the 1960s in rural Pennsylvania.

One summer evening at about eight o'clock, there was a knock on the door. It wasn't quite dark yet. My dad answered. I went with him to the door and stood hidden behind his legs.

"We think we hit your cat on the road," the man whispered.

"Was it a silver tabby?" my dad asked, and they said that it was.

"She just jumped out in front of us. We couldn't stop the car in time. We have a cat of our own, so we had to come and tell you," the man continued as we walked with him from our front door out to the road.

His wife was standing next to my cat and wringing her hands. My cat was on her side in the grass with her eyes wide open, staring lifelessly. I immediately picked her up and hugged her to my chest. I began to cry.

"We can get you another kitten," the couple said as they tried to console me.

"I...don't...want...another...kitten," I sobbed and tried to take a breath between each word. "I want this one."

I carried Francis into our house and down to the basement. I continued to hug her and had blood all over my arms and face and down the front of my shirt. My dad quickly hammered together a wooden box to put her in. I stood beside him, sobbing quietly.

"Get that dead cat away from your face," he said to me. I'll always remember how harsh those words seemed. It was my first lesson about death. People aren't comfortable around death.

We laid her in the box and buried her under a tree in our backyard. My dad took me back into the basement and washed the blood off me with a garden hose. I continued crying as the cold water splashed over me. It took several years before I got another kitten because I couldn't bear to replace Francis.

I'm sure those people felt the same way that I did when my hounds killed my neighbor's cat. They couldn't bring her back or replace her no matter how much they wanted to.

I knew I made the right decision in adopting Rosie. She wasn't a replacement pet, and she had a long life after her retirement.

Rosie lived until she was fourteen and a half years old. So much for Gil thinking that she would only live six months after I adopted her. She eventually got to the point where her legs would just give out. She couldn't go up and down the steps at our back door without the help of a sling around her back end. I wanted her to have a good quality of life, and losing her mobility decreased that quality. My biggest concern was that I did not want her to be in pain, and I made the hard call to end her life. I said goodbye to the most famous racing hound I ever knew.

Chapter 6

Canine Freestyle Federation

Kit and I joined the Sirius Guild of the Canine Freestyle Federation (CFF) in 2002. Based in Silver Spring, Maryland, they had some members in Richmond. A couple of instructors from Richmond volunteered to come to Hampton to teach some classes. This particular type of freestyle was all about the relationship and bonding of the handler and the dog. There were no costumes for the handler or dog, although the dog was allowed to wear a decorative collar. The dog trotted along to the beat of the music. The emphasis was on the choreography and artistry of the dog and handler team.

When I was training Daisy, I had joined Merrimac Dog Training Club in Hampton, and I continued as a member there to train Kit. The building where the classes were held was an old, shabby warehouse in the industrial area along Pembroke Avenue. The gravel parking lot had many potholes, and sometimes the neighbors were kind of sketchy. The cinderblock building was large enough to set up four dog rings. The members had painted the walls white and purchased horse stall rubber matting to cover the floors. It had heating and air conditioning. While it wasn't the Ritz, it sufficed for dog training.

Marilyn, my friend who introduced me to dog dancing, and I started a freestyle class at Merrimac with Kay, a CFF judge from Richmond. She was a petite woman, and her Jack Russell terrier, Ebbie, was a splendid match for her. Ebbie sat and tucked herself into Kay's crossed legs at the beginning of their routine. When they moved around the ring, it was as if they were one being. I was so excited that she was going to be our teacher.

We scheduled the freestyle class early in the evening before the other training classes started at the club because we used music for the routines. The music disturbed the other obedience classes, so we had to be finished before they started.

The first thing Kay wanted to do was to pick a piece of music for Kit. One of the other constraints that the CFF put on their routines was that the music had to be instrumental. I walked Kit around and around the ring to different pieces of music while Kay and Marilyn watched how Kit and I moved together.

"Listen to this piece of piano music from 'Moon River,'" I said to Kay as I popped my CD into the boom box. I had my heart set on it. I felt like Kit and I were floating around the ring as it played.

"It doesn't fit her gait," Kay said. She placed a different CD into the player, and we continued moving around the ring. "This trumpet version of 'Mack the Knife' really accentuates her footsteps." I gave in to Kay's choice because she was the expert.

Marilyn had a petite pug named Buckwheat that she had rescued. Kay found an old song from the 1980s called "Hot Butter, the Popcorn Song." The synthesizer music that sounded like popcorn kernels popping was a perfect match to the funny, jumpy way Buckwheat had of moving across the floor.

Kit and I began to work on our choreography. The beginning of the routine was called an opening shape. I placed Kit in a sphynx-like down, and I stood at the end of the lead from her. When the music started, she would stand up and then start moving in a heel position, staying close beside me with her front shoulder almost touching my leg. The beginner levels of canine freestyle were done on lead, and higher levels were performed off lead. I always worried about having a greyhound off lead. I thought she would leave my side and run out of the ring. Because Kit was on lead, my choreography was limited. I had her spin beside me and circle me. When she circled me, I had to quickly switch the lead from hand to hand behind my back. She sidestepped beside me too. At the end, I had her lay back down in a similar position to our opening shape.

I poured my soul into training Kit. So much work and commitment went into perfecting our routine, but the payoff was watching the audience react to our dance. I practiced it repeatedly, and each time felt as thrilling as the first time. Kit would look up at me with a soft gaze and her mouth slightly open, almost in a smile. When we were moving around the ring, she would wag her tail. The relationship Kit and I built always amazed me. I was so proud of her. I was so proud of us.

I set my sights on entering a competition. The Sirius Guild was holding a CFF competition at the Rockville Recreation Center near Short Pump. The first dances were starting at eight o'clock in the morning, so we had to arrive early. Just as the sun was beginning to glint over the treetops near the rec center, I pulled my van into the parking lot. I suppose my mind was elsewhere as I opened the back of my van and took some folding chairs and tote bags out. Kit seized that opportunity to jump out of the open hatch. I was in complete panic mode thinking she would bolt into the surrounding woods. Kit hadn't lived with me for very long, and although I had done months of training with her, she did not have a solid recall. The drive to Short Pump was a couple of hours long, and I'm sure she wanted to do some zoomies and stretch her legs. Zoomies were a greyhound's way of displaying joy by running frantically in circles, but sometimes the circles would get larger and larger until the greyhound ran off.

My heart was pounding as I looked her square in the eye. "Do not run away from me," I told her in my most authoritative voice.

She bowed down with her tail wagging furiously. She looked up at me with a mischievous glint in her brown eyes.

"Do not run away from me," I repeated, but this time through clenched teeth.

She looked over her shoulder toward the woods but made no move to run that way. I slowly and calmly walked up to her and grabbed her collar before she bolted. I heaved a sigh of relief. I did not want to call Gil and tell him I lost my first greyhound while en route to a dog dancing competition.

Marilyn arrived soon after that with Buckwheat, but when Kay arrived, she had some bad news.

Turning to me, Kay said, "One of the judges had to cancel, and I have to substitute for that judge. It would be a conflict of interest and unfair to the others if I judged your routine. You understand, don't you?"

"I do understand," I said. I have to say after the scare Kit gave me when she jumped out of the back of the van, I was a little relieved that we didn't have to perform that day. It would have been my first time to work with her in front of a critical audience. Instead we could treat it as just a good socializing experience for Kit to hang out with other participants and to be exposed to a day of music routines.

"Will I be ineligible for you to judge too?" Marilyn asked Kay.

"I helped you pick your music, but you choreographed your own routine. So I think it's okay for you to compete," Kay said.

Marilyn and Buckwheat went on. She ended up getting a first-place ribbon in Level 1 with the "Hot Buttered Popcorn" routine. Buckwheat was adorable and the crowd favorite doing his spins and sidestepping. His little tongue seemed to pop along to the music as he gazed up at Marilyn throughout the routine. He made comical snorting sounds as he huffed along. Kit and I cheered from the sidelines.

After this, Marilyn and I were hooked. We proposed having Carolyn Scott, a United States Canine Freestyle star, come to Merrimac for a two-day-long training seminar. Carolyn and her golden retriever, Rookie, set the bar for canine freestyle. Their routine to "You're the One That I Want" from *Grease* was an internet sensation and had millions of views on YouTube. I was awed by the performance! Carolyn wore Sandy's femme fatale outfit of black spandex pants and a black t-shirt with bare shoulders as she sashayed to the music. Her golden retriever was exuberant with his high-stepping, twirls, and spins. His tail never stopped wagging. We wanted to learn all her tips and tricks. We contacted her in Texas to schedule a date and time.

Carolyn suffered from polio as a child and was always self-conscious about one of her legs, but her dog Rookie gave her confidence to step out and dance in front of millions of people. "Attention, Attitude & Imagination" was the title of our seminar. It was well received within our dog club. Twenty dog and handler teams registered to attend, which seemed unusual for the novel topic. When there were so many other training seminars on dog sports like agility and obedience where the handlers could spend their money, I was delighted that we had such interest. It made me want to dance even more.

Carolyn liked freestyle to be lively and entertaining. She founded her organization called the Musical Dog Sport Association, which highlighted the bond between the dog and the handler.

After our seminar, I changed my routine with Kit completely. I thought since she was a retired racer that didn't get a chance to earn money at the racetrack, I would incorporate that into my routine. When I heard the O'Jays song "For the Love of Money," I knew it was the one. I got Kit a bandanna with a print of one hundred dollar bills on it, and I wore a gold shirt with a pocket square in the shape of a one hundred dollar bill. Kit would spin around me and pirouette on her own. Soon Kit realized that song was hers, and she was ready to perform when it came on.

I was no dancer, but I tried to teach myself a few things about choreography by reading books on dance and studying videos on YouTube. I found I didn't have to choreograph the song from the beginning to the end. I started with portions of the music that we moved to most easily. Then I threw in the transitions where we moved from one position to another. Sometimes if Kit just stood still in a part of the ring while I was several feet away from her, it was more memorable than a flashy move.

The local newspaper, *The Daily Press*, wrote a feature on our dog dancing class. Kit and Buckwheat were the stars of the story. There was a photograph in the paper of Kit standing at attention in the mirrors that were mounted on the walls at Merrimac. My sleek greyhound girl had come a long way from the racetrack. We both had gained so much confidence from dancing together.

Chapter 7

Easter on Parade

Each year, Richmond had a festival on Easter that was called, appropriately enough, Easter on Parade. But it wasn't a parade in the traditional sense. The people themselves were the parade. They held the festival on Monument Avenue, a picturesque street lined with vast mansions and apartment buildings. Monument Avenue was originally named for the six monuments honoring Confederate military heroes and one statue honoring Richmond tennis star Arthur Ashe. There was a grassy median between the two directions of the avenue, which was closed off between Allen and Davis streets for this annual event. The Robert E. Lee statue towered over the Allen Street end, and the festival stretched four blocks away to the Jefferson Davis Memorial. After protests in 2020, the statues on these monuments were toppled, and all that remains are the graffiti-splattered pedestals. But for the years that we attended the festival, people and their dogs promenaded in their Easter finest up and down the avenue. Booths showcasing Richmond's non-profit organizations and some craft vendors lined the median. Greyhound Pets of America (GPA) had a booth every Easter.

I didn't mind volunteering to help GPA with this event because Easter had never been an important holiday for me when I was growing up. My brothers and I had Easter baskets every year, but we didn't go to church. The most outstanding childhood memory I have of Easter was the year that I found the egg with a gold star on it at an Easter egg hunt at my elementary school. The teachers and staff had hidden real dyed eggs, not plastic ones. The prize for finding the egg with the gold star was a chocolate bunny. I almost traded the egg with the gold star to another girl in my class because I thought the eggs that she had were brighter colors. A teacher overheard me and said, "You don't want to do that! Keep that egg with the star!"

But the "stars" of Richmond's Easter on Parade were the characters. Donald and Bryan, called The Bonnet Guys, wore pastel clothes and platform shoes and paraded in elaborate, 3-foot-high Easter bonnets in bright pastel and neon colors. Christopher was a clown on stilts. His red-striped pants, bright yellow shirt, red bowler hat, and purple hair could be seen above the crowd, and people clamored to get photos taken with him, me included. It wasn't Easter until I got my photo taken with Christopher. A petting zoo with lambs, chickens, goats, bunnies, and a miniature horse was popular with the kids, and Peggy the Clown rode a bike blowing bubbles along the way.

A group of Morris dancers, a form of English folk dancing, always pleased the crowd. Mostly made up of men, the group stepped to the rhythm of the music while wearing brightly colored sashes and jingle bells attached to their shins. It was part of the celebration to banish the darkness of winter and invite the warmth of spring. They performed up and down the avenue.

It was in this festive atmosphere of clowns, dancers, and jugglers that different non-profit groups tried not only to get the word out about their organizations but also to take in a few donations.

GPA held a bake sale at their tent, and they also had donation vests made for the greyhounds that resembled the silks they wore when they raced. They were of different colors and had clear plastic envelopes on the sides. I put one on Kit and walked her through the crowd. She collected several dollar bills and even a twenty dollar bill, but one savvy young boy, about five years old, was not interested in playing along.

"I'm not going to pet your dog," he said to me.

"That's okay. You don't have to pet her if you don't want to," I said.

"I'm not going to pet her because it costs money to pet her," he said. "And there are lots of dogs here that I can pet for free."

No amount of explaining on my part could convince him he could pet her for free if he wanted.

A highlight of the event was a Pet Easter Bonnet Contest emceed by Gil and local radio DJ Kat Simons. The radio station supplied all the prizes. The first year that I helped with the contest, the prizes were fabulous—concert tickets and a weekend at a dog-friendly bed-and-breakfast. Dogs and owners registered at a tent manned by my children and me. My son, Eric, and I enjoyed running the registration booth because we had a front-row seat for people watching all day long. We also were located right across the street from the corn dog and lemonade vendor.

During the day, as we passed out the registration numbers, we were serenaded by the musical acts on the stage behind us. There was a grassy area in front of the music stage, and I used that to practice some impromptu dog dancing whenever a song came on that moved me. There were always some onlookers who applauded at the end of our performance.

But much of the time at the registration booth, the conversations went like this:

"Where are the port-a-potties?"

"Go down one block and turn left," my son would say.

As part of our duties, we gave out competition numbers, similar to bib numbers for running races. At three in the afternoon, I would begin lining up the dogs and their owners under the Robert E. Lee statue. The dogs paraded across the stage in front of the crowd and a group of judges. Gil and Kat would ask contestants about their bonnets and costumes. Some years there were only a dozen dogs while other years there were 100. Usually, one veterinarian, a city official, and a representative of one of the animal non-profits comprised the group of judges.

Although the contest was called a "bonnet contest," the owners and their dogs turned it into a costume contest. There were dogs with their fur painted to look like Easter eggs. There were matching dog and owner outfits. One owner added some olive-shaped pillows to one of those plastic conical collars on her greyhound and she looked like a martini. And of course, there were dogs with fantastic bonnets. The contest was for all pets, not just dogs. One year, the audience was treated to a chicken, a bearded dragon, and a pot-bellied pig that the owners pushed to the stage in a baby pram.

One elderly man with long gray hair and beard came to the pet bonnet contest every year. He wore a ball cap, a faded blue t-shirt, and jeans. Accompanying him were two overweight black labs, Lil Bit and Blanca, that he dressed in pink t-shirts with oversized pink sunglasses. One year, after he showed up for several years without winning, the judges must have felt sorry for him and gave him the winning vote.

"First place goes to Lil Bit and Blanca!" Gil announced.

The eccentric old man coaxed the two overweight labs up onto the metal stage, but when he was handed the gift card to PetSmart, he shook his head.

"I don't want that credit card," he said to Gil. He seemed to have a paranoid fear that somehow the government could track him if he accepted the card.

"It's not a credit card. It's a gift card. For pet supplies," Gil replied.

"I'm happy I won. But I don't want the gift card."

"Okay," Gil said. And he gave the gift card to the golden retriever in a tutu with pastel Easter eggs on it who came in second place.

The last year that I helped with the contest, it was not so much fun because Gil and Kat were no longer emceeing the event. The contest was still a big draw for the festival. A crowd of thousands made their way to the Lee statue to watch. The company that ran the whole Easter on Parade event sent only one person to run the bonnet contest, and she also had to be the emcee. My son, Eric, ran the registration. I lined up the dogs to go on the stage.

With our meager staff, we were not prepared to handle any situation above our bonnet contest duties. A young woman who was either drunk or had some form of mental illness was determined to get on the stage. She was dressed in blue jean shorts, a t-shirt, and hiking boots. She carried a tall, carved wooden hiking stick.

My son gave the competitors their race bib numbers. As I lined them up, I put them in numerical order. I would call out, "Numbers 100 through 110 I need you to line up here to get ready to go on the stage. Number 100, you stand here. Number 101, you stand here." And so forth.

This woman, who was wielding the large walking stick but had no Easter bonnet, no costume, and no dog, repeatedly came up to me. "I'm number 312. When do I get on the stage?"

"Go get your dog. Come back, and I'll put you on the stage with the 300 group," I said.

She would leave for a few minutes to mill around the crowd, and then she would be back. "I'm number 312. I need to get on the stage." Still no dog. And she had that big stick. I got worried.

I motioned for the emcee. "You need to call someone in security about this woman." The emcee was the only person around from the event company. She didn't have a backup person to help her out.

"I don't have a number for anyone in security. This is the first time I've done this. I didn't even know I had to emcee the event," she whispered to me.

"Go and get your dog," I again said to the woman. She left, and we got through putting the rest of the dogs on stage. The judges were deliberating when she returned.

"I'm number 312, and I need to get on the stage," she said in a much louder voice, clearly agitated. Still no dog.

"The contest is over," I said. "But let's go talk to the judges."

Luckily one of the judges was a city official who worked in social services and had some experience dealing with troubled people.

"Miss, write down your name, phone number, and your bib number on this piece of paper," he said. The paper was just a scrap that the judges used for note-taking during the contest. "I will make sure you get your chance to be on the stage."

That seemed to satisfy her, but she continually mumbled, "I'm number 312. I'm number 312. I'm number 312."

With the contest over, the crowd started to disperse, and she disappeared with her hiking stick into the crowd. I heaved a sigh of relief that her behavior didn't escalate into a more serious problem.

The judge called me over and said, "Joyce, we looked up the phone number that she gave us, and it's the phone number for Chicago Animal Control. 312 is the Chicago area code."

"Maybe she lost a dog in Chicago and was trying to tell us that?" I wondered out loud.

"I guess we'll never know," the judge replied.

Eric and I finished with our duties and began packing up to go home. We took down the canopy tent and rolled it to my car. We took a last-minute walk around the festival area and got some corn dogs to eat.

I had hoped that at some point we could do a dog dancing demonstration at Easter on Parade to complement all the other dog activities, but that never materialized. I did snippets of routines with Kit here and there, and the spectators seemed to enjoy watching it. But I was never able to get a group of dog dancers together to make it a real part of the overall event. Dancing with dogs was such an important part of my life; maybe I was as irrational as the 312 girl, but I wanted all the people that I came into contact with to feel the same way.

Chapter 8

Motley Crew

Because I had completely changed my routine for Kit, and because I found that there were no local groups of the Musical Dance Sports organization, I joined the World Canine Freestyle Organization (WCFO). They had two types of freestyle: Musical Freestyle and Heelwork to Music. In Musical Freestyle, any moves were allowed as long as they didn't harm the dog. Those included jumps, weaves, and send-outs, a move where the dog ran away from the handler and waited in another part of the ring. In Heelwork to Music, the dog and handler stayed in proximity to one another and moved as one unit. The dog spun, turned, and pivoted next to the handler. The big difference between WCFO and the other organizations I had belonged to was that in WCFO one could choose costumes for both the handler and the dog, which coordinated with the theme of the music. World Canine Freestyle events had Olympic-style scoring similar to pairs ice skating. Scores comprised fifty percent for technical merit and fifty percent for artistic impression.

I was never a dancer when I was growing up, far from it. When I was a young child, I thought everyone's mother was the same as mine. My mother worked at the Tel-Star Inn, a bar. Initially, we thought her schedule would be great for our family. She wouldn't start her shift at the bar until 10:00 a.m., so she would be at home with plenty of time to wake me and my three brothers for school every morning. My dad came home from work at four thirty, so we would only be home after school by ourselves for about an hour. My mom would get off work at 7:00 p.m. and be home to tuck us into bed. But as she started drinking more and more, that practical, advantageous scenario rarely happened. Most days, she would drink when she got off work and not come home until the bar closed at 2:00 a.m. She would pass out and not wake up in the morning to get us ready for school.

My father became the classic enabler. He worked two jobs to supplement the income lost from my mother's drinking. Most of the time, my brothers and I were on our own.

I was the middle child and the only girl. In the late 1960s, household chores were female responsibilities. Chores fell to me. When I was eight years old, I would push a kitchen chair over to the stove to boil a pot of water to cook spaghetti for our dinner and then push the chair to the sink to do dishes afterward. I helped my dad do all our laundry on Sundays when he had the day off. We had one of those wringer washers and laundry tubs in the basement. The clothes would agitate in the washing basin, and then we'd put them through the wringer into a tub of cold water to rinse.

"Don't put your fingers too close to the wringer!" he cautioned me, repeatedly.

I would have to dunk my hands into the ice-cold rinse water and repeat the process so we could hang the clothes to dry on lines strung across our basement. Blue jeans and flannel shirts were so heavy when they were wet.

We had a cistern at our house for everyday uses of water like the laundry and flushing the toilets. Every Sunday, my dad and I went to a spring in the side of a hill where we filled up jugs for our drinking water. There was always work to do.

Sometimes my mother would go missing for days at a time. "Don't tell anyone at school that she's not here," my dad would warn.

I found solace in animals and books during this time. I loved to read to escape to other worlds. I didn't have many friends, although occasionally I would bring home a stray cat or dog. Sure, they were one more responsibility, but when you're eight years old and helping to take care of a family of six, what is one more? Those animals filled an empty longing in me.

When I was growing up, we didn't keep pets inside our house. We lived in a rural area of southwestern Pennsylvania and animals lived outside. We fed them but we didn't spay or neuter them. When I was eight years old, I got a puppy from one of our neighbors. I picked a male so I wouldn't have puppies to try to find homes for when he was old enough to breed. He was a small sable and white collie mix, and I named him Tippy because he had a small bit of black hair on the tip of his tail. He was great company.

At the time, my parents were involved in stock car racing. They went to car races at the local racetrack, Heidelberg Raceway, a half-mile oval dirt track a few miles south of Pittsburgh. They dragged me along to races every Friday night. I hated it. When the cars would start around the track, there was so much dust in the air that I could barely see. And the noise was more deafening than any airport, causing me to spend most of the night holding my hands over my ears. My mom loved the drivers Herb Scott, Buddy Baker, and Norm Benning, Sr.

At about the same time as Heidelberg featured some NASCAR races, my parents decided they were going to Daytona Beach to watch the Daytona 500 in February. About a week before the trip was scheduled, Tippy got shot in the front leg by some unskilled deer hunter.

I steeled myself because I thought my dad would just take him to the woods and finish the job, but for some reason, he took him to the vet. Because the bullet had gone straight through his leg and only nicked the bone, the vet could sew him up and put a cast on his leg. I couldn't leave Tippy and go to Florida when he was injured.

I was relieved when my mom arranged with one of her girlfriends for Tippy and me to stay with her for the week. I put a plastic bread bag over Tippy's cast and walked him out in the snow every day.

My mom's girlfriend had a grown daughter who didn't live with her anymore, so I got to stay in her room. I remember it being painted pink, with the most beautiful canopy bed and plush pink carpet. Each day, the woman would make breakfast, pack a lunch for me, and take me to school. I felt like I had hit the jackpot. I didn't have to go to the race, I got to take care of my dog, and this woman was so nice to me.

Near the end of the week, I felt brave enough to tell her how my mom neglected us.

"Don't you ever say anything like that about your mom again," she scolded me. "Your mom is the nicest, most generous person I know."

And I didn't tell any outsiders about my mom's drinking ever again. I took care of my dog, and I kept my mother's drinking a secret for many years. Tippy was my companion dog, but I didn't train him. He was always by my side.

As was the fate of many animals in rural Pennsylvania, Tippy got hit by a car and was killed. When he didn't come home for feeding for several days, I searched and searched for him in the woods behind our house, calling his name over and over. My dad was the one who noticed the skid marks on the road and found Tippy's body in the ditch. We buried him next to my cat, Francis.

Fast forward to Kit again. I wanted to train her, and I also wanted to teach Canine Freestyle to others so we could have a group to do demos and competitions. When I was a young girl, besides having a soft spot for dogs and cats, I always liked languages and writing. I found it fascinating that people spoke other languages. I suppose if I could have picked an ideal job for myself, it would have been working in the publishing industry. I would have loved to become a translator and translate books into other languages. I took some German classes in high school, and I tried to teach myself French with some online software and by speaking with my friends when we visited France.

One reason I loved dog training was that I was communicating with another species. That just blew my mind. Dog training took communication to the next level. Dogs and humans didn't speak the same language, but somehow the dogs understood me. There was a bond between me and the dog, but I must give credit to the dogs. They were the ones who did most of the understanding.

Marilyn and I put together a motley crew of dog dancers to do demos and competitions. Let me tell you about the crew. Pat owned a modeling and talent agency and had been a model herself. It was such a dichotomy to see her with her frumpy English bulldog, Deezel. His bottom row of teeth stuck out from under his lip. He waddled when he walked, and he would do anything for Pat. We choreographed a routine for them to the song, "Bad to the Bone." Deezel wore a leather jacket, and he was so comical. Everyone loved it! Tami, my friend who introduced me to Willow, danced with her black and white Olde English bull terrier, Diamond. The Olde English bull terrier was a mix of a bulldog and a Boston terrier. Tami was so pretty with her long blond hair and long legs. She always looked so pulled together. Diamond wore a pink tutu for her routine to "Mony, Mony" by Tommy James and the Shondells. Leslie and her Swiss mountain dog, Curly Sue, had a cute routine to the theme song from the television show *Hill St. Blues*. Leslie wore a denim shirt and a newsboy cap. Another star of our show was another woman named Pat with her beautiful papillon, Nike. The music Pat chose was an instrumental piece called "Homecoming." She created an elaborate routine that included a hoop festooned with flowers for Nike to jump through. The haunting melody and the precise movements of that tiny dog brought tears to the eyes of the audience.

To become a better instructor, I attended a WCFO workshop and competition at an indoor soccer sports complex in North Carolina. It was a week-long workshop with classes every day, and it culminated in a two-day WCFO competition.

I volunteered to be the gatekeeper at the competition so I would have a front-row seat to all the routines.

Gary Wilkes, a behaviorist and dog trainer who was instrumental in introducing clicker-based training in the United States in the early nineties, was a presenter. He taught that both reinforcement and punishment were required to clearly communicate what a dog needs to do and what they need to stop doing. I took Kit to his workshop session, and she had something to say about it.

Kit was always a whiner. When left alone in her crate, she whined. She whined when asked to lie quietly during a workshop session. She whined when I wasn't paying attention to her.

One of Gary's methods of shaping unwanted behavior was the "bonker." The "bonker" is a bath towel, folded up and rolled to about a four-and-a-half-inch diameter, secured with a rubber band. When an animal exhibits a behavior that the trainer is trying to diminish, the trainer says "no," and then bonks the animal with the towel. The idea is to create an unwanted or undesirable consequence for the behavior. An example for humans might be if you stepped out the front door and always stepped into a mud puddle, then you would find another way to exit your house. In other words, you would change your behavior because you did not want the consequence.

As Gary was explaining the "bonker" to the group, Kit began to whine, so I gave her treats to stop her from whining. Gary soon called me out on that.

"What are you doing?" he asked in front of all the workshop attendees.

"I'm trying to keep her quiet so that you can talk," I said, red-faced.

"You're treating her for whining. You're reinforcing her unacceptable behavior," he said. "Just let her go. Let her whine."

He continued with his explanation of reinforcement and punishment. Kit continued to whine. Soon he shouted, "No!" The towel flew and hit her on the crown of the head. She immediately stopped whining. There were audible gasps from the attendees.

Wilkes explained that the marker word "no" pinpointed the bad behavior, and the bonker was the consequence of whining. Kit would work to avoid that behavior in the future. It immediately took her mind off what she was doing. Then he instructed me to treat her when she was quiet because she needed to get clicks and treats for correct behavior. After about twenty minutes or so, she began to whine. He yelled, "No!" and the bonker flew again.

By the end of the workshop, she was lying quietly in her crate.

When I left the class, I had several other attendees approach me in dismay. "I would NEVER let someone else hit my dog like that" was what most of them said, but the towel didn't hurt her. She did eventually quit whining, so the technique was successful. Still, I could never bring myself to hit her with a towel. Sometimes it's hard for us to accept that learning can't always mean yummy treats.

Maybe if I had said no and bonked my childhood dog, Tippy, with a towel when he ran toward the woods, he would have never run off to get shot and would have never been hit by a car. But I didn't have that experience when I was a young child. Once I learned more, I showed more understanding and became a better freestyle instructor for it. As a child, I felt so different, but dog training and dog dancing allowed me to be bold enough to stand out, even in my motley crew.

Chapter 9

Nursing Home Therapy Dogs

A colleague of mine from the lab attended a physics conference in Florida. There he met a woman computer scientist at one of the lunches who took her dogs to a nursing home as therapy dogs. When he explained to her that he knew a woman, me, who taught her greyhounds to do dog dancing, she asked him if he thought this dog dancer would be interested in coming to northeastern North Carolina for a weekend to teach a workshop to her therapy dog group. As the conference drew attendees from around the world, my colleague was surprised to find out that the computer scientist lived relatively close by.

When my friend returned from the conference, he told me about the woman he met.

"Joyce, I met this woman at the conference, and over lunch, she started telling me about her dogs," he said.

"Everyone always tells me about their dogs, even if I don't want to hear about them," I joked with him. I had a sign on my cubicle wall that said, "Dogs Welcome, People Tolerated."

"She showed me pictures of two little terrier-type dogs, one named Lady and one named Waldo, and a Newfoundland named Brutus. I had never seen a Newfoundland before, and I'm telling you, if there was ever a dog look-a-like contest, she would win with that Newfoundland. She was short and heavy with dark brown hair, almost black hair. Big brown eyes. She also seemed kind and good-natured—and that's how she described her Newfoundland. I think you would really like her. She does therapy work with her dogs. I told her I would give her your email address if that's okay with you."

"That would be fine," I said. "We call Newfoundlands 'Newfies.' What's this lady's name?"

He handed me a business card with Margaret's name on it.

Just as my colleague had said, Margaret was kind, gentle, intelligent, and good-natured. After emailing her a few times, we made plans for me to teach her group some dog dancing. I found out through our email conversations that only her terrier-type dog named Waldo remained. Her other two dogs had died.

Alan, Kit, and I headed for North Carolina on a Friday evening. Margaret had invited us to stay at her home.

"We can stay at a motel," I said. "I don't want to put you out."

"No, you should stay with us. But I want to warn you that my house is kind of messy. I'm not the best housekeeper," she said. That didn't bother me because I'm not the best housekeeper either.

But when we walked into her split-level house, I was shocked. There were piles of papers and clothes everywhere, with only a small path to get from one room to another. The kitchen counters were piled high with dirty dishes and dusty stacks of old mail, catalogs, and magazines. One cabinet door in the kitchen was hanging askew from one hinge.

We walked into the living room and sat down on the edges of a couch and a chair where she had cleaned off a small section for us. Kit squeezed onto a small space on the floor beside me. The coffee table was piled with old mail, and there was a line of drool marks on the wall at the height of her Newfie's head. I imagined him shaking his head and the drool flying, spattering the wall.

She said, "I made dinner for you. Eggplant parmigiana and french fries. We can't eat in the dining room because the table is a mess. And there is a spot on the carpet in there where my old girl, Lady, had an accident. And since she passed, I can't bring myself to clean it up. You understand that, don't you?"

I could see tears forming in Margaret's eyes as she talked about Lady. I shook my head yes, but I'm not sure I understood. I guessed it was the same as not cleaning the drool marks off the wall. We held the plates on our laps to eat, and it was all I could do to suppress my gag reflex and to swallow.

After dinner, she showed us downstairs. There was a living room, bedroom, bathroom, and a separate entrance.

"Usually we rent this out, but we just lost our previous tenant. We haven't found anyone to replace him yet, so that works out for us. You have a place to stay for the weekend," she said.

Hanging on the wall, I noticed several short swords, a mace, and a crossbow. "Oh, my husband participates in LARP games, and those are his weapons," Margaret explained, following my gaze.

"What is LARP?" I asked.

"It's live-action role-playing. It's kind of like Dungeons and Dragons but with real live people who portray their characters instead of game pieces on a board. There's a Game Master who keeps the game moving. The characters battle with each other, and that's what the weapons are for. It's quite complicated. He's at a game right now at one of our parks. Maybe he can tell you about it this weekend sometime."

We got ready for bed and discovered that we had no control over the thermostat. Margaret told us she kept it cool at night for sleeping. It was about 58 degrees. Alan didn't like to let Kit sleep on the bed, so I slept with her on the couch in the downstairs living room. It was more of a three-dog night, but I only had one dog. I regretted we didn't just stay at a motel. I was so cold that my teeth were chattering, and it was summertime.

In the morning we got up and found that Margaret's husband had bought some glazed doughnuts for us to have with our coffee. The box was balanced precariously on a stack of unread mail on the kitchen counter. We had our coffee and headed for the hospital.

Kit had to wear her yellow plastic turnout muzzle in the hospital because she wasn't one of the therapy dogs who had been tested by an evaluator with the hospital. We went upstairs to our designated training area in one of the lobbies. I had my boom box, a bag with CDs of various songs, treats, and water. Lots of heavy items to carry. I was glad Margaret had a little Red Flyer wagon to transport all our articles.

We met with two other ladies who did therapy work with their dogs at the hospital. I began the class by explaining that we would start by picking music for everyone. Margaret had her terrier, Waldo. One woman who joined us had a golden retriever and the other a whippet. Margaret expected more people, but those were the only ones who showed up. The first hurdle in teaching a class is that everyone has an idea about what kind of music they want to use, and it rarely fits with the gait of their dogs. I did it myself the first time with Kit.

After some friendly debate, we found a piece of music for everyone, and I gave them their opening shapes. The opening shape was supposed to look like a painting. The handler and dog held the pose for ten seconds for the audience to get a picture in their mind. Then the handler and dog break into their movement.

I started working with them to teach their dogs the tricks they needed for the beginner level: right turn, left turn and backing up. The dogs circled the handlers as they heeled. Some dogs and handlers spun simultaneously. Others could jump over the handler's arms and legs. Sometimes just having the dog stand still was a good move. With this repertoire of movements, the handlers created some nice routines for their dogs. These dogs were already trained as therapy dogs, so it wasn't difficult to add in a few movements they would need for dog dancing.

We took a break for lunch. Margaret ordered salads for us from some local restaurant, and we ate them outside in a courtyard.

After lunch, we put everyone's routines together. I would write the movements and draw a map on a piece of paper to show the handlers what they had to do with the dogs. The map resembled those old *Family Circus* comics in the newspaper with the thick dotted lines and arrows to show one of the cartoon kids' paths through the house or the neighborhood. The maps were quite helpful to remember the routines. If they were ever going to compete, they would have to use a certain percentage of the floor or ring space. Since they were performing at the nursing home for their residents, they needed to take up a much smaller space, like a lobby.

We finished the workshop in the afternoon and asked the nurses if some of the patients would be interested in seeing our routines. They thought that was a wonderful idea.

About a dozen patients in wheelchairs and some of their family members circled the lobby area. Margaret and her friends each performed their minute-long routines. At the end of the golden retriever's performance, his owner knelt, and he jumped over her back. That move was met with enthusiastic applause. Kit gave the performance finale with her theatrical "For the Love of Money" routine.

After seeing all the patients' smiling faces, I was pretty sure the golden retriever's owner was convinced to look up WCFO and to start competing. She was hooked. All in all, it was a successful afternoon.

We returned to Margaret's house, and I was relieved to hear she wanted to go out for dinner. We left Kit in a crate in the downstairs apartment. She was exhausted from the day. I wished I had brought a blanket to wrap her in though. We went to one of those Brazilian steakhouses for dinner. There was a little wooden dowel on the table, painted red on one end and green on the other. If you wanted the server to bring you more food, you turned the green side up. While you were eating, you turned the red side up. And the waiters with big knives kept bringing the meat to the table on big skewers—chicken thighs, filet mignon, pork loin, lamb, huge chunks of sausage, and bottom sirloin sliced into long strips. It was the first time we had ever eaten in a place like this, and we didn't pace ourselves.

As the knives flew up and down the skewers right beside our heads, Margaret's husband told us all about LARP warfare.

"I usually attend the day games, but some of my friends go on weekend camping trips. The first time I was attacked by a couple of crunchies, I was fanatical about it," he said.

"What is a crunchie?" I asked.

"Crunchies are nameless creatures who dress up in monster costumes and paint their faces just to fight with you," he answered animatedly. "I love swinging a sword or an ax at them, even if the weapons are made of foam. You're not allowed to hit them too hard though."

"Uh-huh," I nodded. I hoped my less than enthusiastic answer would be enough to end the conversation.

We slept fitfully that night because we were so full and still cold. We could hardly wait to get back on the road the next morning and head for home. Too many swords and crossbows for me to want to stay one more night.

A few weeks later, I received a letter from the hospital. Inside was a crayon drawing of Kit and me. Kit was drawn with a body like a sausage with toothpicks sticking out for legs. Her head was egg shaped with pointy ears. I was drawn as a stick figure, but the head had hair that resembled mine and glasses where the eyes should be. Both of us sported enthusiastic red smiles. Some short, curved lines next to our legs showed some dance moves. One-inch-tall, scratchy blue letters spelled out "Thank you." The accompanying letter from one of the nurses explained that this young girl had been visiting with her grandmother on the day we were at the hospital. She asked the nurse to send it to me. I was moved by the drawing, and it made the whole uncomfortable weekend worthwhile.

Chapter 10

My Poor Girl

I first noticed that Kit had flaky skin. She was a black dog, so it was very noticeable. Her whole underside seemed to be flaking off. I tried feeding her some extra fish. I always used salmon as a treat for her because she loved it so much. She would drool when the salmon came out. I thought if I gave her even more fish, the oil would help with the skin.

But then she started having some diarrhea and losing weight. I took her to my vet, and he ran some bloodwork on her. Her stomach was very tender to the touch. Her protein levels were very low.

When the bloodwork came back, the vet called me at work in alarm. He said her albumin levels were so low that she needed to be seen by an internal medicine specialist vet as soon as possible. Albumin is a protein that forms in the liver and is carried into the blood. It regulates the blood volume by controlling pressure and retaining fluid in the veins. If she had advanced liver disease, fluid might build up in her chest and lungs, and her heart might stop working. My vet gave me the number to call in Virginia Beach.

When I called, the receptionist said that my vet had already called to inform them of the emergency. Kit probably wouldn't last more than a few days if I didn't bring her in right away. My hands were shaking when I hung up the phone.

I told my boss I had to leave right away to take my dog to the vet.

I drove home, picked her up, and went directly to the specialist's office, which was about a forty-five-minute drive from my house. I had to cross over the Hampton Roads Bridge-Tunnel, which is notorious for trapping traffic. Thankfully, not that day!

I got to the office, which was located near a small serene lake, but there was nothing serene about our emergency visit. I got Kit out of the car and took her for a short walk next to the lake to see if she had to go to the bathroom. I know that dogs absorb our emotions, and I attempted to smile on the outside for her while my stomach fluttered on the inside. I tried to take some deep breaths, and then rushed her inside.

The vet explained to me he was going to sedate her and do an endoscopy on her. He could tell if her liver was shutting down or if there was some other problem. I had to leave her there for the afternoon and could pick her up around their closing time of four in the afternoon.

Because I was on the other side of the bridge-tunnel from home, I decided I would go to a restaurant to get something to eat, and a glass of wine to calm my nerves. But when I went outside to my car, I couldn't find my car keys. I had been in such a hurry to get her inside the vet's office that I thought I must have dropped them somewhere. I went back inside and talked to the receptionist.

"Has anyone turned in a set of car keys? I seem to have lost mine," I said. I was biting my lip so I wouldn't cry.

"No one has turned anything in," she replied. "Maybe you can retrace your steps."

When I walked out of the office to retrace my steps, I was in tears. I drifted slowly through the parking lot with my head down, looking for something shiny that could be my keys. I walked over to a tree by the lake where I had let Kit relieve herself before I took her inside. I fanned my feet in arcs as I searched through the grass. No keys. I thought to myself, "I'll have to call Alan and have him bring over another set."

I went to sit in the car to use the Tracphone that I had only for emergencies. And there were the keys in the ignition. I had been in such a hurry to get her into the office; I didn't even take the keys out of the ignition. I guess I was lucky that no one stole my car while I was inside.

I went off to a restaurant to sit by myself and think about my poor girl.

At four p.m., I went back to pick her up and talk to the internal medicine vet. He said that her whole intestinal tract was inflamed, and she had inflammatory bowel syndrome. The protein wasn't being absorbed into her system because her intestinal tract was so inflamed.

He prescribed a large dose of steroids to try to reduce the inflammation in her intestines. He suggested I change her food to a prescription kibble for digestive health and add in a probiotic supplement powder. No extra treats to give her stomach a rest. She was very sick.

The steroids seemed to make her very weak and thirsty. Then she would drink a lot of water and need to urinate more often. We had three steps leading up to our back door and when she went outside; she struggled to get up those three steps to get back into the house. The vet had shaved her front leg to insert an IV while doing her endoscopy and that hair never grew back.

Canine freestyle would have to wait now. I had to concentrate on getting Kit well. I loved canine freestyle. I loved teaching it. I loved seeing the dogs get so excited when they danced. It made me happy. But I couldn't dance with a sick dog.

For the next couple of months, I took her on short walks, but she didn't have the strength to do much else. Her muscles seemed to be breaking down. That elegant greyhound body was failing her.

One particularly frosty night in January, my husband and our neighbors had reservations to go to a wine tasting dinner at a local restaurant. Ever since our boat trip on the canal through France, we jumped at any chance to do wine tastings. But my intuition told me I shouldn't go. I insisted they go without me.

Kit kept wanting to go outside, even with the frigid temperatures. So, I let her out. She didn't come back to the door asking to be let back inside. Later in the evening, I went looking for her. She was lying behind the shed. She had gone outside to die.

With tears in my eyes, I knew it was time. I loaded her into my car and drove to the emergency vet's office to have her put down. By that time, around midnight, she was too weak to even stand. The vet techs came outside with a gurney, lifted her from the back of my van, and took her inside. They laid her on a blanket on the floor of one of the exam rooms.

I sat cross-legged with her on the floor and held her head in my lap. She didn't even look up at me as the vet put in the shot. She was ready to go.

"Thank you for being my dog," I whispered in her ear.

I came home with only her leash and collar.

I blamed myself for keeping her alive longer than I should have. I could have put her down a lot sooner and saved her from suffering. I failed her. I thought I was stronger, but I couldn't do it. It was selfish of me. I know that. But I also blamed the vets. They offered one idea after another to keep her going. I just kept thinking if I did the next thing and the next thing that the vet suggested, she would suddenly get better. And I would have her around for a longer time.

Grief is difficult. My daily routine changed without her there. I was used to letting her in and out of the back door to go to the backyard. I missed hearing her dog tags tinkling. I swear that one day I opened the back door, and I felt her brush by my legs.

I knew I missed Kit, but I also knew I would get another greyhound. It's part of the recovery process. She wouldn't have wanted me to be by myself with no dog to love.

My grief at losing this dancing dog reminded me of the loss of my mother. My mother was an alcoholic and unfit to parent in many ways. Despite this, I felt sad when she passed. I was 24 years old when she died.

She died as a result of a fall. She came home drunk one night from the bar and fell out of her car. The doctors thought the fall dislodged a blood clot in her knee that traveled to her brain. During the night when she was sleeping, she had a stroke. My dad said that he heard a gurgling sound coming from her and he called an ambulance. My dad called me, and I met them at the hospital.

A nurse in her room was keeping her breathing with a blue manual resuscitating plastic bag. The doctors talked to us and said they could operate on her, but she would never be the same. There was too much damage.

"She wouldn't want to be alive hooked to a machine," my dad said.

"Once we stop helping her breathe, she won't last long," the doctor said. "Only a few minutes. You should call the rest of your family to say goodbye."

I went to a payphone in the hallway to call and tell my first husband, Dale. My husband and I had been going through a rough patch in our marriage at that time. We lived in a different area code than the hospital, so I needed more than a dime. I rummaged through my purse to collect all the change I could find.

I dialed the number and put in the coins.

"Hello," Dale said.

And I froze. I couldn't speak. No words would come out of my throat.

"Hello? Hello?" he said a couple more times.

I made a little squawking sound. I couldn't breathe. I started to cry. I wanted to say, "My mom is dying."

He hung up on me.

I stood in the hallway holding the phone receiver in my hand and cried for a while cursing silently.

I had to find more change in the bottom of my purse to call him back and explain what was going on. This time I was able to get the whole story out. He apologized for hanging up on me, but our marriage didn't last.

My brothers arrived shortly after that. My dad called the minister from his church who was a woman. I felt my mom would have liked that. We stood in a circle around her bed and held hands. We were all afraid to touch her. The room was silent except for the whoosh of the nurse squeezing that plastic bag.

The pastor said that my mom was going home, and she wanted to let her know that she would have a smooth transition. She wanted my mom to know that in this difficult time her family would be all right. She asked us to bow our heads as she requested God's strength for us. She recited the 23rd Psalm. The pastor nodded to the nurse, and she took the resuscitator away from my mom's face.

We slowly filed out of the room after that.

The nurse, in a low voice almost like a whisper, said to us, "I need one of you to stay behind and collect her jewelry."

"I can't do it," my dad said immediately. He wiped tears from his eyes.

"I will," I said, stoically.

The nurse unclasped the gold chain from around her neck. And then slowly twisted off her diamond engagement ring and wedding band. This wasn't like the movies. I watched my mother slowly turn blue as all of this was happening. I took the jewelry in one hand, and I reached out to touch her arm with the other hand. It was cold and hard and felt like I was touching a piece of plastic. It didn't feel like I was touching another person. I didn't cry.

"She's not here anymore," the nurse said to me. "This is just a shell."

My mom died just two days before she was to turn 48 years old. For her birthday, I bought her a compact turntable with speakers from Sears to play her vinyl records and to replace her wooden console stereo that recently quit working. I wanted to surprise her.

A week after her funeral, I returned the stereo to the store. I thought I was fine. I took the box up to the customer service counter.

"Can I help you?" the clerk smiled and asked.

"I'd like to return this stereo," I said.

"What's wrong with it?" she asked matter-of-factly.

"I ... bought ... it ... for ... my ... mom's ... birthday. But ... she ... died." I sobbed and took a breath between each word. I couldn't help myself and I couldn't stop crying. I didn't even cry that hard at the funeral.

"I'm so sorry," the clerk said. She quickly started processing the return to get me out of there as quickly as she could.

I regained my composure. "No, *I'm* sorry," I sniffled. "I don't know where that came from." I was crying for all the years I wanted a mother, and she wasn't there for me. I was overwhelmed and didn't even realize it. The poor store clerk just happened to be in the wrong place at the wrong time.

Finally, the tears stopped coming and then I could explain to her how I bought the stereo, we were going to have a birthday party, my mom had this sudden stroke and didn't make it through, and I had to return the stereo.

She returned my money and again said how sorry she was.

Losing Kit was just as devastating to me as losing my mother. Kit gave me constant companionship while my mother was never reliable. Even though I had time to prepare for Kit's death and my mother's death was more of an accident, both deaths were intense. But my relationship with Kit was simple. She was always there.

Chapter 11

Things People Say to Greyhound Owners

What kind of dog is that?
   Is that a greyhound?
   If that's a greyhound, why isn't he grey?
Does he run fast?
Did he race?
Those are beautiful dogs.
If I had dogs that ugly, I'd never take them outside.
Is that a Great Dane? He looks like a Great Dane. Are you *sure* he's not a Great Dane?
Is that a groundhog? I mean, greyhound?
I thought you were walking a tiger.
Oh, I saw you from across the park and I thought you had a goat.
If that dog stood up on his hind legs, he would be taller than me!
Did you know there's a drink called a Greyhound? Vodka and grapefruit juice.

He looks like an anteater.
Look at the muscles in that butt!
Why are his teeth chattering? Is he cold?
Does he need a lot of exercise?
I've heard they're very high strung, is that true?
Is that a whippet?
Are greyhounds dumb?
Can he live in an apartment?
Did you rescue him? God bless you for that.

Chapter 12

A Greyhound Puppy?

In the greyhound racing world, the dog's pedigree is important. Greyhound fanciers have recorded this information for four centuries in the United Kingdom. The oldest pedigrees go back to 1790. There is a huge online database where one can search for littermates and race history.

But sometimes there can be an "oops" litter due to accidental breeding. Dogs can be ingenious when they want to breed. If the female is bred and the breeder doesn't know which male was the stud, then the litter can't be registered to race. When this happens, sometimes the whole litter is culled. Sometimes the litter is given to a farmer who can use the dogs to hunt coyotes. And sometimes the litter is given to an adoption group so they can find homes for the puppies.

Greyhound puppies are not born with the temperament of the older retired racers. Breeders keep racing puppies with their littermates for twelve to eighteen months. They are socialized and trained to become the calm animals that most greyhound adopters know. Not so for greyhound puppies who haven't been raised this way.

One day I got a phone call from Gil. There was an "oops" litter in Florida. One of the other GPA-Richmond adopters was getting one puppy from the litter, and Gil wondered if I would like to have one too. He sent me a photo.

The foster parent had taken the photo from above. In it, this young hound, about three months old, was lying next to a sliding glass door with his huge brown eyes looking upward and a neon yellow tennis ball nestled between his feet. The photo just made me go "Aww." The pup was white with brindle spots, what the greyhound fanciers call particolored. He was all legs and tail and triangle-shaped head. To me he looked like a marionette—one where the puppeteer couldn't quite control the strings, so the legs went one way and tail went the other way. In the middle of his forehead, he had what I called a "smart mark," a little spot of brindle coloring within the white. His foster family was calling him Sammy.

I thought it must be fate that his name was Sammy. I was going to train him to become a dog dancer, and his name would be Sammy Davis, Jr., the namesake of the talented tap dancer.

Can one fall in love with a photo and a name? I did.

"Have him transported to Virginia," I told Gil. "I'll take him."

"I'll bring him along to the picnic, and you can pick him up there," Gil said.

Every year, the GPA had a group picnic at a park in Richmond. The picnic was a way for the adopters to meet each other and to get together with their hounds. There was a potluck lunch and some greyhound games to play. Someone brought a police radar gun used to measure the speed of moving objects. The dogs ran down a chute made of orange construction fencing and were timed to see who still ran the fastest. There were contests for the longest tail and the baldest butt, and raffles to win gift baskets. An ice cream social ended the day when all the greyhounds got vanilla ice cream sundaes with crushed pieces of colored milk bones on top.

Because I was a dog trainer, I usually came up with the games and contests. I did a lot of timed wrapping games. The owners wrapped their dogs in toilet paper to look like mummies. They wrapped them in green crepe streamers and decorated them with stickers to look like Christmas trees. They wrapped them in red, white, and green crepe streamers to look like the Mexican flag for Cinco de Mayo.

I also copied a lot of game shows. We played a *Concentration* type of memory game. I purchased two greyhound calendars and attached the twelve photos to poster board. I laid the poster board on the ground. The people had to walk with their greyhounds through the giant game board on the ground and turn over the boards. If the pictures matched, the dog-handler team got a point. The dog-handler team with the most points won.

We had race games where the handlers would have to hold a large spoon with a tennis ball in the bowl of the spoon in the same hand as their leash. To win, they would run to one end of the field and back again without dropping the tennis ball from the spoon. The favorite race game was one where there was a basket of clothes at one end of the field, and the dog and handler had to run to the basket, pick out an item of clothing, put it on their dog, and then run back. They had to do this three times, and the first one to complete an outfit won the game. On the first run, they had to put a piece of clothing like a shirt, pants, or skirt on their hound. On the second run, they had to put on an accessory like a party hat, necklace, or tie. And on the last run, they had to put on at least two socks. It was comical watching the dogs trying to run with socks on their feet. The dog would take a step, try unsuccessfully to shake the sock off his foot, take another step, and repeat the shaking with the other foot. Afterward, we had a fashion contest to award the best overall costume.

A memorial service to those beloved dogs who passed away was a somber part of the picnic. Grieving owners said the names of their hounds out loud among other greyhound owners who could support them. I hung my head and said Kit's name. Gil would then burn a collar from one of the missing dogs.

There was always a group "roo" at the picnic. The "roo" is a siren song that greyhounds make, a combination of a whine and a howl. Once one dog started, they all joined in. This cacophony of voices drowned out any fire trucks or ambulances in the area.

At one of those picnics, I walked up to the picnic pavilion, and there was Gil's son, Alex, holding Sammy in his arms. Sammy was wearing a tiny lime green collar. His legs were sticking straight up in the air, and his long tail was curled down toward the ground like a treble clef on a staff.

"Here's your puppy," Alex announced.

As soon as Alex put him down, he barked. Not the sweet singing sound of the "roo"—but a yappy, annoying bark like a seal begging for a fish at SeaWorld. Something we tell people who are going to adopt a greyhound is that they don't bark. They are terrible guard dogs because they never bark. Someone can enter your house and take your television set, and maybe they will lift their heads from where they're sleeping and look at the burglar, but they won't bark at him. Sammy was not the typical greyhound in that regard. When he was awake, he was barking.

By the time Sammy arrived, both of my children were adults and had moved away from home. They still got upset when I called Sammy my fur kid and them my skin kids.

I took Sammy home with me and started his training. My friend Marilyn was giving training lessons at the house of our friend Pat, who owned papillons. Pat turned her garage in Poquoson, Virginia into a small training building. She put green mats on the floor and had a small heating and air conditioning unit installed. It was big enough to hold four to six dog-handler teams at a time. I started training Sammy to be a STAR puppy.

STAR is an acronym for Socialization, Training, Activity, and Responsibility. It is a six-week program developed by the American Kennel Club that focuses on various skills for both the owners and the puppies. The owners learn about routine vet care and to clean up after their puppies. The puppy learns how to behave around other dogs and people.

The responsibility part of the STAR test required owners to always pick up their puppy's poop. Owners were supposed to always carry plastic bags in their pockets. I learned a trick from Marilyn, and that was to invert the bag over my hand, scoop up the poop, flip the bag back onto the poop, cover it with the bag, tie a knot in it and throw it in the trash. Voilà, no poop on the hand. But I did one better. Since the greyhounds were so tall, I just stuck my plastic-covered hand under them while they squatted. The poop never hit the ground.

People who saw me perform this function had various reactions. One day I was walking the dogs at the beach, and a little boy watched me do this.

He said, "You pick up their poop with your hands? You NASTY!"

I think if I left the poop on the sandy beach for him to step in, that would have been nastier.

A man that saw me doing this on the beach while driving by in his truck near the boardwalk stopped and said, "I don't know what you're doing, but you're a good person for doing it." Then Sammy kicked some sand in my face. No good deed goes unpunished.

Another time a woman saw me, and she said, "You trained your dog to poop into a plastic bag? That's genius!"

Although the classes helped, Sammy was still extremely hyper. He rarely slept, chewed anything that he could get his teeth on, and the barking never stopped.

One evening, as I returned home from walking Sammy, Alan was sitting in his recliner, but the television was uncharacteristically silent and black. He held out his hand to show me some black plastic shards, some squares with numbers, and a few colored wires.

"Do you know what this used to be?" he asked.

"No," I answered.

"It used to be the controller for our TIVO. I looked online, and it will cost sixty-five dollars to replace it. And in the meantime, we can't watch tv."

Sammy and I tried to slink away into the bedroom to annoy him no further.

But Sammy's chewing went from bad to worse. One day I came home from work to find the remains of a book chewed up on the floor. The spine was completely gone.

For Alan's fiftieth birthday party, I asked that if anyone wanted to give him a gift, they could gift him a copy of their favorite book and inscribe in the front why it was their favorite. Alan's boss gave him a first edition of *Admiral Hornblower in the West Indies* by C. S. Forester. His boss inscribed it as follows: *Dear Alan, When I was young, I read all of C. S. Forester's books. In fact, I am reading one of them now—it is called* The General. *I was particularly enamored with the Hornblower series—the sea and the exploits of a sailor during the Napoleon Times. I believe it was that interest that led to my first career of ships and my love of sailing.*

The inscription was still intact, but the edges of the pages had teeth marks like a shark had bitten its prey. Of all the books on the bookshelf, Sammy had to pull that one out. He could have chewed up a James Patterson or Danielle Steele novel that I could have easily replaced.

I had to fess up to Alan.

"Sammy chewed up one of your birthday books," I said.

"Which one?"

"The one from your boss," I said as I held the carcass of the book out for him. "I'm sorry."

"You really need to crate that dog," Alan fumed. Sammy was not his favorite greyhound.

Even though I didn't know how to stop him from chewing up inappropriate objects, I continued Sammy's dog training with the hope that we would make some progress, and he passed the Canine Good Citizen test.

Then I began to teach him the basics of canine freestyle. When he was learning, he wasn't barking. We started with heeling and weaving. I knew from dancing with Kit that the more commands and tricks that he knew, the more elaborate our routines could be. I also knew that I would be giving him commands from many different positions, not merely when I was standing still beside him. We progressed to spinning on both the right side and the left, circling me, and jumping over my outstretched arms and legs. The more we practiced, the stronger our bond became. Maybe he wasn't Alan's favorite, but I was falling in love with my little puppy.

Chapter 13

James River Greyhounds

In addition to training Sammy for freestyle, I continued my work with the greyhound adoption group. The group changed hands and names again. Gil stepped down from running things, and a couple of new people took over, Mark and Trina. They moved away from Greyhound Pets of America, and the group became James River Greyhounds, which continued to be a dedicated group of volunteers who wanted to find suitable homes for the ex-racers.

One task for me, besides the home visits, was to pick up any hounds that the owners no longer wanted. That was written in the adoption agreement—if the owner didn't want the dog for any reason, they would return the dog to James River Greyhounds rather than take the dog to a shelter or re-home the dog themselves. We called these dogs bouncebacks.

One Friday, Mark called me and asked if I could pick up a dog named Nikko in Poquoson, Virginia.

"I usually go out to dinner at the Thai restaurant on Friday evenings. Fri-day, Thai-day," I told him. "But I can pick the dog up sometime over the weekend."

"These people are adamant they want the dog out of the house tonight," he said.

"I guess I could go by after dinner," I told him.

At around 7:00 p.m. when we finished with dinner, Alan and I drove to the apartment in Poquoson. A thirty-something woman in a tank top and sweatpants answered the door when I knocked.

"Oh, I'm so glad you're here," she said. She had the crate, a dog bed, and a plastic container for kibble in her foyer. Nikko, a young female, white with fawn spots, was lying quietly on the couch.

"This dog! She never stops barking! She barks and cries all day and all night. We're about to get evicted from our apartment. We crate her during the day while we're at work. We had to buy a padlock for the crate because she bent the door by chewing on it. She even broke a tooth trying to chew the bars on her crate."

"How long do you keep her in a crate?" I asked.

"Only a few hours," she quickly answered.

I cocked my head and looked at her skeptically. The hounds are so used to being crated at the track. It sounded like the dog had been kept in the crate a lot longer than a few hours at a time.

"She isn't housebroken. She poops and pees all over the house. She has ruined all our rugs," the woman continued. "I just know she's going to get us evicted."

"Okay, you just have to sign these release papers, and I'll take her."

The woman couldn't sign the papers fast enough.

"And take all this stuff. The crate. The food. Her toys. Her coat. I never want another dog for as long as I live," she said with a sense of urgency.

My husband and I loaded all her stuff into my car.

"Come on, Nikko," I said to the dog. She hopped off the sofa and willingly followed me to my car. She jumped up into the back cargo area with no problems. I thought for sure I heard the deadbolt lock on the door of the apartment as we left.

On the way back home, Alan and I discussed what our lives were going to be like with this troublesome dog. We might not get any sleep. We'd have to dog-proof all the rooms by putting up all the things she could chew. I would have to come home from work at lunchtime to walk her so there would be no accidents.

That first night as I prepared for the worst, she slept straight through. Not a peep. I got up in the morning and took her for a walk with Sammy. When I came home from work that day, not a single accident.

I kept her for a week with no problems at all. Mark found a great home for Nikko on the Northern Neck peninsula. Her new people drove to our house to pick her up. They were a retired couple and had an older Italian greyhound mix. Italian greyhounds are the toy version of the greyhound. The couple had recently lost their older greyhound, and the Italian greyhound was lonesome for a new companion. They had three fenced acres for the dogs. Nikko went off to live with them, and we never heard of any troubles with her again. Maybe the first woman who adopted her should never have gotten a dog in the first place.

On another occasion, Mark got a call from a home in Chesapeake where I had placed a greyhound. The man was a police officer, and his wife was a physical therapist. They worked opposing shifts—one worked nights and the other days. They had adopted a black greyhound whom they named Radar in honor of the police officer's work tracking down speeders, but now they wanted to return him.

Greyhounds get something called "happy tail," but there is nothing happy about it. They have extremely thin skin, and whenever they get any kind of nick or cut, it bleeds profusely. When they wag their tails, sometimes the tail hits on something and gets a gash in it. The greyhound continues to wag its tail, and the blood from the gash splatters all over anything in its way—furniture, cabinets, and the wall. You get the picture.

One day, the police officer returned from his shift to find that Radar had a case of happy tail while locked in their laundry room. Evidently, he had nicked his tail on the washing machine. The entire room was splattered in blood. He called to have Radar re-homed. When I arrived to pick Radar up, he said to me, "I've worked a lot of crime scenes and this was worse than any I'd ever seen. There was blood everywhere. I just can't take it."

Unlike the woman who had Nikko, he cried when I packed Radar into my van to take him back to my house. But sometimes the bravest thing one can do is give the dog back when there is a feeling the dog can't be cared for properly anymore. Since Radar invoked this officer's post-traumatic stress disorder, Radar needed a new home.

Black greyhounds are the hardest for the adoption group to place. In the animal shelter world, we call it Big Black Dog

Syndrome. Adopters overlook black dogs in shelters in favor of lighter-colored animals. There are several reasons for this, none of them very scientific. People associate the color black with evil or bad luck, like the superstition of having bad luck if a black cat crosses your path. Radar had the double obstacle of being a black dog and not being cat safe. I called him a big black cat zapper. This fact limited his potential adopters to those who didn't have cats or small dogs in their homes.

First, I drove him to a home in Charlottesville, Virginia. I'm always amazed at what people will tell me and show me when I'm doing a home visit. This man took me outside to show me his two dog boxes. One dog box had a border collie chained to it.

He said, "This is my border collie. And this other box here is where I'm going to chain my greyhound."

I thought to myself, "Not this greyhound!" But politely I explained to him that greyhounds could not be kept outside. They have no body fat and can't survive in extremes of cold or hot, not to mention that they couldn't be chained. If a squirrel or rabbit ran past, the hound would break its neck trying to run after it. I told him that a greyhound was not a good fit for him. I felt so sorry for his poor border collie.

My second chance at re-homing Radar came from a personal trainer who owned a gym on the Eastern Shore of Virginia. He wanted a dog to take to the gym with him. I told him Radar had the perfect temperament for a shop dog. He was very calm and would probably lie behind the counter and not bother any of his clients as they worked out. I drove Radar there to meet him. I had to go through two bridge-tunnels to cross the Chesapeake Bay—not a short drive for me. When we arrived, he took one look at Radar, who was a black dog whose muzzle had grayed out, and said, "He just doesn't fit the image I want for my gym. He's not virile looking. He looks so old. Don't you have another dog that looks a little bit younger than this one?"

I thought to myself, "Of course, we have younger-looking dogs. But I wouldn't give you *any* greyhound now. They're not decorative elements for your gym business!"

As I was driving home through the traffic of the two bridge-tunnels, I decided to keep Radar. I thought he was a beautiful dog. He had the gray muzzle which I affectionately call muzzle sparkles, but he was only five years old. The saying goes that one dog year equals seven human years, but that's not entirely accurate. The first year of a dog's life equals fifteen years. The second year equals about nine years. And every year after that equals four to five years. At most, Radar was the equivalent of a thirty-nine-year-old man. He and the trainer at the gym were probably the same age. Radar had a short mane on his neck and communicated his emotions like a horse. I read on the *Greyhound Data Forum* that the mane comes from greyhounds bred in colder climates like Ireland. It was the gym owner's loss and my gain.

Chapter 14

Hit the Road, Jack

The first dog dancing song I choreographed for Sammy was to "Hit the Road, Jack." It matched his gait, and I liked it a lot too. Why? It was the first tap song that I learned at a "legitimate" dance school.

Two of my girlfriends who I worked with at the lab thought a dance class would be a great way for us to get together once a week and see each other. We decided to take a tap and jazz dance class. I had just turned fifty and had never taken a dance class in my life. As I stated before, my childhood was less than ideal, and taking dance classes was not a priority. I liked the idea of seeing my friends more, but more than that, I thought the class would be a great way for me to become a better dog dancer.

One of my girlfriends contacted the dance school owner and asked, "Two of my girlfriends and I would like to start taking the adult tap and jazz class. Would that be okay?"

"Well, it's already December, and the classes started in September. The women in the class are already preparing their dance for the recital in May," she said.

"We're not professional dancers. We just wanted a fun thing to do once a week. It's not like we're headed to Broadway."

"If you stand in the back and don't bother the ladies who are working on their recital dance, you can join," the dance school owner said. We were in.

How I loved that class! Tammy was the most wonderful, enthusiastic teacher. She taught the class a few simple tap combinations to the song "Hit the Road, Jack," and then she would squeal, "Look! You're dancing!" and "We have choreography!" When I flapped, slapped, and brushed with my tap shoes to that song, it filled me with joy. She motivated and inspired me.

When I couldn't quite get a step right, she would say, "Just do as you are able." I tried to give myself just the right mixture of challenges to keep myself inspired, but I was not so adamant about doing the steps that I would be too hard on myself when I couldn't do something difficult like a toe cramp roll. Two steps right, then left, then two heel drops, but the first two steps are on the toes like a ballerina en pointe, and the result is the sound of a galloping horse.

Tammy was about five foot, six inches tall and had long brunette hair with blond highlights that she kept in a bun during class. She majored in dance at college. Like a bee, she never stopped long in one place. She wore black dance sneakers that had a plastic sole in two parts, so she made little light tapping sounds as she moved around the floor. She had a celebrity crush on country singer Keith Urban. A picture of him on her attendance book, propped up under the barre, was our audience during class.

As much as I enjoyed the dancing, what I relished and cherished was getting together with the six women in my class. We were all of different ages, from our twenties to our fifties. We shared all the milestones: birthdays, heartbreaks, deaths, new babies, new jobs, weddings, and divorce. We supported and encouraged each other. They became my tribe. That dance class changed my life in so many ways. Not only did it make me a better dog dancer but also I could be the child I never was allowed to be.

I never had a lot of girlfriends when I was growing up mainly because I was embarrassed about my home life. I didn't want anyone to find out about my mother and her drinking. I always felt like an impostor.

When I was in the seventh grade, I skipped a grade in school. While all the kids in my neighborhood were taking earth and space science and basic math, I was taking biology and geometry. When they took biology, I took chemistry. When they took chemistry, I took physics. And it went on like this throughout high school. There was a group of about thirty of us in this gifted class, and we stayed together throughout high school. But I never felt like I belonged to the gifted class either. I thought at any moment that someone was going to figure out that I wasn't smart enough and didn't belong there.

But this group of dancing women made me feel like I belonged. I shared secrets with them. I never did that with anyone else before. I felt safe with them. They held me up with their close friendships. I had so few woman friends in my life that I didn't have bridesmaids at either of my weddings. And now I had some of the best friends ever.

The two youngest women in the class, Sarah and Julia, were cousins. Julia, the older of the two by a few years, was a nurse. She had long blond hair and blue eyes. Sarah was a hairdresser with medium-length brunette hair and beautiful brown eyes. Van Morrison probably had her in mind when he sang "Brown-Eyed Girl." Sarah had taken dance lessons at the dance studio from a very early age.

Julia and I were the plus-sized girls. We didn't have the typical long and lean dancer body type. It didn't affect our dancing, but it was a little problematic when it was time to choose costumes for the recitals. Many dance costumes did not come in plus sizes. I had the added problem of being very tall, and Julia was much shorter. The rest of the tribe was never judgmental though. They would pick something from the limited choices, and we always seemed to look fabulous.

Susan was a beautiful blond navy wife. She had four children—three boys and a girl. Her husband was the commander of a ship, so their family moved around a lot. She was very active with the other navy wives, making sure families were settled when they moved from place to place. Her parents lived close to the dance studio though, so that area would always be her home. Her daughter also danced at the studio and was in the color guard at her high school. Susan was not only a dance mom but also a band mom.

Becky, a close friend of Tammy's, was a nurse with three children. Her husband was one of the local veterinarians. Becky had been a majorette in high school so sometimes Tammy choreographed a dance with a cane as a prop for Becky to twirl. She had extremely short black hair, and I had short red hair. We were always the ones who worried about hairpieces and hair accessories that came with the costumes.

Sandy was my girlfriend from the lab, who instigated the whole dance night out. Sandy had shoulder-length blond hair and blue eyes. She had been a cheerleader in high school and never lost that athleticism. She did cartwheels wherever we went, and she wowed the audience in our first recital when she did a split for the finale of our dance. Even though we both worked at the lab, we hardly ever saw each other because we worked in different buildings on the campus. We tried to go out to lunch once a month, but that didn't always work out. This dance class was a sure method for us to see each other each week.

Last but not least was Lesa. She became one of my best friends, and I was always pinching myself about that. One of Lesa's hobbies was decorating her house. In my house, I had mismatched furniture with bedsheets for covers on the couch so the dogs wouldn't mess it up. I didn't think she would find anything that I did interesting. Still, we both loved New York City, and maybe that was enough for her. Lesa had long dark brunette hair. She also had been a cheerleader in high school and had taken ballet lessons most of her life. She had one daughter who also danced at the studio. Lesa had a Boston terrier named Butler, and our mutual love of dogs became a keystone of our friendship.

Something I shared with Sandy, Becky, and Lesa, as they had been married longer than the others, was the effect of my husband's inherited genetic disease on my relationship with him. Alan had ankylosing spondylitis (AS), an inflammatory arthritis that mainly affects the spine but also spreads to other joints. His back movement became limited as the vertebrae in his spine fused. The cartilage in many of his joints became calcified. This began happening when he was in his twenties, and it progressed throughout his adult life. His rib cage stiffened, and he found it harder and harder to breathe. Not only was he in constant pain but he also began to panic when he fell asleep. It was so difficult for him to breathe when he was lying down that he was afraid he would go to sleep and not wake up.

AS is also known as bamboo spine when the vertebrae fuse. Early treatment for the condition was to take anti-inflammatory drugs like NSAIDs and steroids. These treatments then caused other problems like kidney disease. It was a balancing act for Alan to control the pain without compromising his other organs.

Being in constant pain made living as husband and wife not very pleasant for Alan. As our intimacy fizzled, I felt we were just going through the motions. We held hands, and we kissed goodnight, but not much more than that.

At first, I was hurt by it. Finally, I realized I was lonely. I was in this long-term relationship, but there was such a longing there. Even though we lived in the same house, I felt we had drifted apart. Sometimes it was even lonelier than if I had no one else because it wasn't like I could get into another intimate relationship. I loved my husband.

I was less lonely when I was surrounded by Lesa, Sandy, Becky, and the rest of the dance ladies. I confided in my tribe. But overwhelmingly, just the nearness of my little particolored greyhound, Sammy, filled a void in me that no one else could. It is so fulfilling when animals give us that unconditional love. I threw myself into Sammy's training. We traveled together to workshops, dog dancing competitions, and training classes. He provided companionship for me because he was so loyal and affectionate.

I felt happier when I was with Sammy, and I tried to bring the fun we had to our dance classes. I always talked to the ladies about my dog dancing, and they had their own ways of keeping the class lively. When we got stuck trying to come up with some choreography, Julia would pretend she was playing the saxophone in a marching band and would recommend that as a move. Once a year we got ribbons and trophies on awards night, and Becky would exclaim, "This is the BEST DAY EVER!" Connecting with these women gave me energy and satisfaction.

Lesa and I tried a different dance studio one year when, for some reason, our original studio didn't have an adult tap and jazz class. We did enjoy tapping at the new place once a week, but I would have appreciated it a lot more if the teacher hadn't insisted on using the song "Footloose" for every single warm-up dance. She had a huge folder of CDs that she brought to every class with her. She would begin class by thumbing through the folder looking for a warm-up song.

"What should we dance to? What should we dance to?" I could hear her ask herself under her breath. "How about this one?"

And inevitably, out would come "Footloose."

That is one song I would never choose for dog dancing, no matter how well it matched a dog's gait, because I couldn't stand to hear it one more time.

In 2011, only a year after my first class, I performed in my first dance recital to the "Theme from *New York, New York*." The choice of song couldn't have been more perfect for me. I always wanted to live in New York City, and this song was my anthem. Also, it was the song that Jabba and Sandra performed in the very first video I ever saw about dog dancing.

The costumes, however, were a different story. The owner of the studio chose silver-sequined leotards with a black tuxedo front. They were beautiful, but as older students, we didn't quite feel comfortable performing for an audience in leotards and tights. At the last minute, the studio owner said she would order some black pants to wear over the leotards.

It was Susan who first tried on the pants. They were dragging the floor like flippers on a seal, and the waist was so huge that two dancers could have fit in them.

"They're clown pants!" Sandy exclaimed.

"What are we going to do? The recital is in a week," Tammy said as we were all laughing at the comical pants.

I tried my pants on, and even though I am five foot, ten inches tall, the pants dragged on the floor by at least six inches. What kind of a dancer would have ever worn those pants? Marilyn came to my rescue. She hemmed the pants and took in the waist, and I had them in time for the dress rehearsal that Friday night.

By Saturday's performance, we all had our costumes in order when we arrived at the Ferguson Center for the Arts, even down to our white gloves. We had a Rockettes-like kick line at the end of our dance, and the crowd went wild.

When I was leaving the center after the performance, a woman from the audience approached me.

"You are so brave to get up there and dance like that. You were wonderful," she said.

"Oh, anyone could do it," I said, but inside I was beaming.

Chapter 15

Pet Crazy

I took Sammy to a WCFO competition in Fredericksburg, Virginia to try out our new routine. As the competition was held in February of 2012, it was called the Presidential Puppy Prance to honor Presidents Day. When I arrived at the venue, I found out the competition was being documented by a producer from the ABC news show *20/20*. They were doing an episode called "Pet Crazy," and one segment was on dog dancing.

As I set up my folding chair and Sammy's crate in the waiting area, the producer introduced himself to me. A handsome, dark-haired young man in jeans and a sport coat, he seemed out of place in the room full of costumed women and their dogs.

"Hi, I'm Chris, a producer from ABC's show *20/20*. Do you mind if I ask you a few questions and take some video?" He shouldered a tripod and a video camera.

"Not at all," I said.

He seemed to enjoy Sammy's antics from the start. Sammy nudged my hand to get treats from me. He stood behind me and poked his head out from either side like a young child playing hide and seek. Chris laughed when Sammy curled up on his bed beside me but looked up at me and barked like he was talking to me. The barking!

"What kind of dog is that?" he asked.

"He's a greyhound adopted from the racetrack, although I've had him since he was a puppy. He's the second greyhound that I trained for dog dancing," I explained.

"How do you train them to do dog dancing?" he asked.

"You start by training them to do some tricks like spinning, weaving through your legs, and jumping over your arms and legs. Then you put it to music. I started with my first greyhound, Kit, by watching some videos. Then I took some classes and went to a couple of workshops. Kit passed away when she was nine years old."

"I'm sorry," he said.

"They never live long enough for us. But then I got Sammy as a puppy to train. Puppies should be easier to train than older dogs, but as you can see, I have not trained him to be quiet," I laughed.

He followed us around and took video; he even followed us out to the car to take a break from the performances.

"What do you think the dogs are thinking about when they do these performances?" he asked me with the video camera rolling.

"I think they really enjoy it. If you watch them looking up at their handlers, there is joy in their eyes. You can see the tails wagging. I know they remember their training because they know which moves come next in the routine and understand the words, even the words to the songs. Because they'll spin when they hear the word *spin*. They'll sit when they hear the word *sit*. And sometimes they get so excited they throw in their own moves. Because they don't talk, we'll never really know what they're thinking. But if you watch their behaviors, you can communicate with them. That is one of the joys of canine freestyle, bonding with your dog," I said.

He nodded his head.

"Or maybe Sammy just likes gobbling up the string cheese that I give him for treats," I winked.

When it was our turn to go into the ring, I told the producer, "This is my first competition, and I'm kind of nervous. The nerves go right down the leash into the dog."

They played the national anthem at the start of the competition. It always makes me tear up. I hoped the cameras weren't rolling for that.

I wore the silver tuxedo costume from the "*New York, New York*" dance, but I added a black fedora. Sammy wore a black and silver collar. We looked very much like we had just left the Rat Pack of the 1960s.

But looks were not enough. Our performance was terrible! Before, when I had done any dance demonstration with Sammy, I always used a towel or a mat for him to lie on in the ring. The towel would give him a focal point and provided some traction when any floors were slippery. I thought that wasn't allowed in the competition ring because the judges would consider it a performance prop. So when Sammy was supposed to be in a down position at the beginning of our "Hit the Road, Jack" performance, he kept popping up because he wasn't used to lying on the bare floor. A perfect score was ten. (Imagine the judges holding up perfect ten scorecards when Nadia Comaneci delivered her performance on the balance beam or floor exercise in the Olympics.) We received fours and fives.

I didn't speak to anyone as I left the ring. I quickly packed up Sammy's crate, my folding chair, and my tote bag, and headed to my car to escape.

I was hanging my head as we headed back to the motel at the end of the day. Sammy held his head down too. He didn't want to hurt my feelings like this. I wasn't crying, but he knew that I was upset.

I wasn't the only one who was off that day. The black standard poodle kept running out of the ring. A Doberman pinscher concentrated his gaze more on the ring-side person holding a turkey sandwich than on his handler. My friend with the mountain cur spent so much time in the practice ring, waiting for the *20/20* cameramen to leave the main ring, that her dog barely had any oomph left to complete her routine.

That evening it snowed, and when I awoke at the motel the next morning, I considered just packing up my stuff and going home. But I had the chance to do my performance one more time to see if I could improve my scores. I decided to compete with a fresh attitude. Chris and the *20/20* people were gone on the second day, so that made the entire atmosphere a little less intense. The handlers weren't worried about being on camera, and the dogs weren't so distracted.

When I arrived, one of the other competitors had a black and white polka-dotted beach towel she thought she might use during her routine, but then she changed her mind. She asked me if I wanted to use it for Sammy's routine. She had seen our disastrous performance the day before and thought maybe this would help. The black and white fit with the color scheme of our costume and collar.

"That's allowed?" I asked her.

"Yes, as long as it's not used as a reward for any kind of behavior. If all he's going to do is lie down on it," she said.

I took the towel into the ring and laid it down where I wanted Sammy to start. He immediately went into a down position on it. Then he went through a nearly flawless routine. Sammy looked up at me and read my face for clues to what I wanted him to do. When he was supposed to, he circled me. He stopped in place. I circled him like he was the center of a clock and I was at the end of the second hand ticking away. He did figure eights around and under my legs as I leaned right and left. At the end, he went back to the towel and lay down on it, and I fanned my hand to him, like Vanna White turning over the winning letter in *Wheel of Fortune*, just as the last note of the song sounded.

We won first place in our beginner's division. Sammy was awarded a medal and a ribbon. I was so happy we had returned. And when the *20/20* episode aired, Sammy was in one of the introductory clips. The producer had followed me around for several hours, and we had about ten seconds on the air. He aired a few seconds of Sammy barking and then the quip about the nerves and the leash. I felt like an actor who had shot many brilliant scenes for a movie only to see the scenes not make the final cut of the film.

It wasn't long after my spotlight on television that I had my first dance accident at the studio. At the beginning of dance class, we were doing spins across the floor in our jazz shoes. There were crosses of different colored tape on the floor to mark where each dancer stands. (It helps to visualize the distance between dancers.) As I was spinning, my shoe caught on one of the pieces of tape, my foot stuck, and my over 200-pound body kept spinning. I came crashing down on that stuck foot.

At first they laughed, but then several of the ladies rushed to me and helped me off the floor.

"Are you okay?" Tammy called out.

"It really hurts, but I think I'll be all right," I said, embarrassed.

I finished the class. I even changed into my tap shoes and tapped, but when I got to my car, I knew something wasn't right. My foot was throbbing. I headed to the emergency room on my way home. After x-rays, the doctor determined that I had broken the little bone on the outside of my left foot that attaches the pinky toe to the mid-foot. This break is commonly known as the dancer's fracture!

My foot swelled and turned black and blue. The hospital gave me one of those big black moon boots to wear. I hobbled around on crutches for weeks. I had heard of other dancers who continued to dance with a broken bone, but I was not that strong. Sadly, I had to give up tap dancing for the remainder of the year.

In my heart of hearts, I smiled inside when anyone asked me how I injured my foot. It signaled to me that I was a real dancer and this was a badge of honor.

"I was tap dancing!"

Chapter 16

Free Fallin'

Sammy may have been the barker, and I may have broken my foot, but Radar was my accident-prone dog. We lived in a ranch-style, blue-sided house on the Salt Ponds in Hampton, Virginia. Our half-acre yard bordered a marshy area filled with seagrass. We had a small borrow-pit pond directly on the other side of our chain-link fence. We caught blue crabs in the pond by throwing out a chicken neck tied to a string and scooping the crab up out of the water with a net. There was a small sandy peninsula that separated the borrow-pit pond from a small tidal inlet, and people in the neighborhood sometimes came there to fish for croaker and spot. It was private property, and they weren't supposed to do this without permission, but many did.

One sunny morning, I let the dogs outside like any other day. From the kitchen, I heard Sammy barking. A staccato bark, over and over, not like his usual barking. I went outside to investigate.

Radar was lying on his side in the grass, and Sammy was running around him, barking and snapping at him. There was a top and bottom fishing rig attached to Radar in such a way that he couldn't move. One hook was through one of the pads of his back foot, and the other rig was hooked to his tail. He must have run through the yard, caught the hook in his foot, and caused the other hook to swing around and attach to his tail. He couldn't stand up without causing one or the other of the hooks to dig in deeper.

"No, no, no," I kept shouting to Sammy as I cringed at the thought of the pain Radar was in.

Radar weighed seventy-five pounds, but I was determined to pick him up. I carried him as far as the back deck of our house and had to put him down. The whole time I was trying to carry him, Sammy was circling us, barking and snapping like a hyena circling his prey.

I yelled to my husband, who was upstairs in our bedroom, "Alan, come down here!" It surprised me he hadn't already heard the barking and commotion.

He came outside and asked me what happened. I told him about the fishhooks.

He said, "Those fishhooks are barbed so we can't pull them out. The only thing we can do is push them through." He got a pair of pliers, and he managed to get the one out of Radar's tail without too much trouble or pain on Radar's part. But the one in his pad was embedded.

"I can't get that one out," he said. "You'll have to take him to the vet."

Of course, it was a Saturday morning. These kinds of things never happen when the regular vet is open. I had to take him to the emergency vet.

My husband helped me load Radar into the van. At least with the hook out of his tail, he could stand on his three good legs.

Once in the car, I was worried that he would try to lick his foot and get a cut on his tongue. But he just panted, which is a typical response to pain and stress.

When we arrived at the emergency vet, I got him out of the car. We went inside, and they quickly took him to the examining room. It only took about ten minutes before the vet was calling me back to where we could talk.

"I gave him a sedative and a local anesthetic and sliced his pad to get the hook out. He'll have to wear a cone for a few days. I didn't think it needed stitches. I'll give him something for pain, but he'll be fine," the vet said.

I knew it wasn't a life-threatening injury, but I still heaved a sigh of relief.

It was pitiful to watch him enter the house when I got him home. Wearing the big plastic cone that he bumped into every piece of furniture and doorway, he hobbled on three legs and held his back foot up. He was still a little loopy from the anesthetic as he lay down on a futon we had in our spare bedroom. He finally fell into a deep sleep.

After several weeks of recovery, I trained Radar, and he passed the Canine Good Citizen's test and the therapy dog test at Pat's garage training building, but he was never comfortable in a therapy dog role. One of my mantras for dog training was this: "Dogs repeat behaviors they are rewarded for." And sometimes what a person finds rewarding is not the same thing that the dog finds rewarding. I used string cheese a lot as a reward, but what Marilyn and I discovered was that Radar disliked being in the training building so much that the only thing he found rewarding was to get out the door. If I wanted him to do a long stay, all I had to do was let him go out the door when he was finished. After he passed the test, I took him to the library so kids could read to him. He tolerated it, but I don't think he enjoyed it.

I taught him a short dance too. The music I picked for him was Aretha Franklin's "Respect." I chose this song because it was one of the songs used in one of our dance recitals and because I had respect for this dog that got knocked down but always got up again. I started with an opening pose of Radar down on the floor between my feet. I think the security of that position reassured him.

As silly as it seems, I wanted to give Radar a birthday party. I don't know if he understood the gesture, but I wanted him to be included.

When I turned fifty, my daughter Jade turned twenty-one. We both have June birthdays. Mine is June 6, and Jade's is June 1. I decided we needed a big dual birthday celebration, and I thought it couldn't hurt to add Radar to the mix. I rented a large white tent at the Sunset Beach Hotel in Cape Charles on Virginia's Eastern Shore for an outdoor party. I reserved a group of motel rooms so our friends and family could spend the night. Sunset Beach was advertised as a resort, but most of the place had been run down and needed remodeling. The lobby had that 1970s beach decor with fishnets, fake crabs, and sand dollars on the walls. The rooms were clean but had a musty smell. They had a private beach within walking distance of the hotel and our tent. The important amenity to me was that it was pet-friendly, so Sammy and Radar could attend. Every one of my friends who had dogs got an extra invitation to bring their dogs to Radar's part of the party. Marilyn brought her pugs, and Jan brought her collies.

There was one other issue with having the party on the Eastern Shore. To get there, one had to drive over the

Chesapeake Bay Bridge-Tunnel and pay a twenty-four dollar toll. It was like asking my friends to pay a cover charge just to get into my party.

I could easily imagine my friends saying, "I like you, Joyce, but I ain't spendin' no twenty-four dollars just to cross a bridge for your birthday party."

I had the hotel cater a barbecue dinner with pork and chicken, macaroni and cheese, and peach cobbler for dessert. They allowed us to bring our own wine and beer. During my trip on Pascal's sailboat through the canal in the South of France, I drank a Coteaux de Languedoc Picpoul white wine. It was one of the wines that we bought from the lockmasters. Because it reminded me of my French friends, I ordered a case of it to have at my birthday party.

We had two birthday cakes decorated in what looked like white pearls of icing, a huge cake with the number fifty and a smaller cake with the number twenty-one. My cake was chocolate as that was my favorite. Radar got a dog bone with icing on it that spelled out, "Yappy Birthday."

With each new birthday, I tried to put the birthdays of my childhood farther and farther behind me. On one such birthday, when I was probably nine or ten, one of my mom's friends made a cake for me with a Barbie doll in the middle of it. Her skirt was the cake. The friend iced the cake to look like a fancy hoopskirt dress. I wanted to take the cake home when I got it, but my mom wanted to set it up on the corner of Golden Goblet's bar for everyone to see. By the time I got to take the cake home the next day, the icing tasted like smoke and grease.

On my fourteenth birthday, one friend in the neighborhood asked my mom if she could have a surprise party for me. My mom told me about the surprise party plans ahead of time so that I could clean the house. Our kitchen floor had twelve-inch, black and white square linoleum tiles, and the thing I remember most about that birthday was being on my hands and knees, scrubbing those tiles one by one. I didn't have fond memories.

For my fiftieth, I asked each of my friends to gift a poem to me. It could be one that they wrote themselves or a favorite poem they enjoyed. I hired a local poet and entertainer to read the poems out loud at the party. He had trouble with the poems written by friends who spoke French but he mustered through.

Despite asking my friends to write poetry and to pay a toll, a fun group of people showed up. I drank too much and paid for it the next day. I had to get up in the morning and walk the dogs along the beach, but I was so sick. I returned to the hotel room and threw up. I lay down on the hotel bed, a wet washcloth over my eyes, with Radar beside me. I don't know why it was Radar beside me and not Sammy, but it was. Radar felt a special connection to me on that day.

Shortly after this, I took Sammy and Radar to the vet for their annual wellness checkups. Radar had been throwing up for a week, but I thought little of it. I thought I would tell the vet about it when I saw him.

The vet started probing his stomach. "Did he get in the garbage and eat anything?" he asked.

"Not that I know of," I said.

"Did he chew up a toy and swallow a part of it?"

"Not that I know of," I said again.

"I feel something in there. I'd like to do exploratory surgery and see what it is," he said.

I left Radar there and took Sammy home. I got a phone call at work a few hours later, and the vet asked me to come back to the office.

"Radar has a tumor between his stomach and his small intestine about the size of a walnut. If I remove the tumor, his small intestine will be strangled and die. I can't operate on it, so I sewed him back up. We could give him some chemotherapy to try to shrink the tumor." He showed me some pictures they had taken of the tumor. He was right. It looked like a little white walnut.

"No chemo," I said.

"I'd just like to put him down. Before he wakes up from the anesthetic," I told the vet and his technician. I thought about all he would have to go through and the quality of his life. He had an incision from below his chest all the way down his stomach from the exploratory surgery. He'd have to wear a cone to keep from licking the incision, and I remembered how much he hated the cone from his fishhook incident. He would be miserable on the drugs. And who knew how long it would give him? I think I had learned my lesson from Kit. I wouldn't keep a dog alive and suffering just for my sake.

I went back to work, sat at my desk, and cried. That it was only supposed to be a wellness visit kept running through my head.

Radar was only seven years old. His race name was WS Free Fallin'. Like the song, he was free fallin' out into nothing and left this world for a while. He was a bad boy for breakin' my heart, but now he was free.

Chapter 17

Jefferson Lab

Merrimac Dog Training Club held many classes, events, and seminars every year, but it was a club of all volunteers. In any situation like that, some people volunteered all the time, and some people never volunteered but took advantage of the perks the club offered.

Each year they helped put on a dog show at the Hampton Roads Convention Center with Langley Kennel Club. It was a huge undertaking and needed many volunteers. In the front lobby of the convention center, as people were entering, there was a section devoted to non-profit rescue groups. Because I had rescued greyhounds, I helped set up a table for my adoption group.

One year, the dog show also set up a memory garden. Several of the members of Langley Kennel Club trucked in a couple of wheelbarrows filled with dirt and added several potted plants. One of their members crafted markers made from paint stirrers with a small wooden plaque glued to the top. Some plaques were dog houses, bones, butterflies, or flowers. For a donation to the kennel club, one could have the names of dogs that had passed on painted on one of these markers and planted in the dirt. Of course I had to do one each for Kit and Radar. The display was a poignant reminder of how much people loved their dogs. There were dozens of colorful markers amid the flowers.

At our adoption table in the lobby, I let Sammy perform a few tricks I hoped would increase our donations. I taught him to take a dollar bill from someone and place it into a bowl. Young children seemed to enjoy that trick. "Give me another dollar, Mom, so I can give it to the dog to put in the bowl!" And I made some signs on sticks: one had a "YES" painted on it, and one had a "NO." I made up another sign that said, "Ask Swami Sammy any question for a $1.00." I had a little fortune teller's hat for Sammy to wear. People walking by asked him a question, and I would hold up the signs in front of Sammy. If he raised his right paw, it was no. If he raised his left paw, it was yes. Usually, they asked if their dog was going to get a ribbon in the dog show. Sammy would always tell them "Yes."

But after years of volunteering for Merrimac, I was getting tired of the members who didn't volunteer and decided to start a dog training club where I worked.

I started working as a mechanical designer at the Thomas Jefferson National Accelerator Facility, also known as Jefferson Lab, in 1988 when it was just a couple of buildings and trailers on a wooded lot. Jefferson Lab evolved into a campus with sixty-nine buildings on 169 acres of land. How did I go from a little girl in southwestern Pennsylvania to a grown woman working at a nuclear physics lab in southeastern Virginia? The journey took many twists and turns, but each phase was built on the one before.

When I was in high school, my dream was to work in publishing in New York City as a translator. I studied German for four years. I majored in German at Westminster College, but I quit after one year for reasons unrelated to the coursework. My parents thought that college was a waste of time. My dad told me to "learn a trade." I then went to a technical school and learned architectural drafting. My first job was at a vacuum processing company in the Lawrenceville section of Pittsburgh. They made rotary vacuum dryers for pharmaceuticals, freeze dryers for coffee, and autoclaves for impregnating telephone poles with creosote. They had a flood, and all their drawings sustained water damage. This was before computers, and because my handwriting was so nice, they hired me to re-trace the damaged drawings. In doing that, I picked up some knowledge of the vacuum processes.

After a couple of years, I applied for a job at Leybold Vacuum Products. They were a German company building a plant in the United States to manufacture their vane pumps. In simplest terms, a vane pump compresses air inside a chamber to create suction. I started working there, translating German drawings into English drawings. I worked there for several years, and besides the translations, I helped design some custom vacuum systems for certain customers. Later, I moved to Virginia and got a job with one of the shipbuilding design companies designing waste and oily waste systems for navy frigates.

One day I saw an ad in the help wanted section of the newspaper for CEBAF. CEBAF was an acronym for the Continuous Electron Beam Accelerator Facility, the precursor to the Thomas Jefferson National Accelerator Facility,

Jefferson Lab. The ad said they needed designers who knew vacuum, cryogenic, and magnet systems. For my entire career up to that point, I had only worked on a drawing board with mechanical pencils.

CEBAF, later called Jefferson Lab, turned into a state-of-the-art nuclear physics laboratory run by the Department of Energy. There the other designers introduced me to a CAD system. CAD stood for Computer-Aided Design. I designed the mechanical components for one of the experimental halls using a three-dimensional modeling system. I designed structures, superconducting magnets, and cryogenic piping and target systems. Everything designed there was one of a kind and had to work correctly the first time. It was challenging work.

I met my husband, Alan, at CEBAF/Jefferson Lab. When I first met him, I didn't like him very much, to put it mildly. It was a more visceral dislike. He was one of the men who interviewed me for my job. When I answered the ad in the newspaper and got called in for an interview, I told my boss at the shipbuilding design company that I was going to the dentist for a checkup. I didn't realize, and no one from Human Resources told me, that the interview was going to take all day. I thought I would be gone for an hour or so. When I arrived at the lab at eight o'clock in the morning, the Human Resources representative gave me my itinerary with interviews lasting until four o'clock in the afternoon.

Each interview got more and more difficult. At one of the first interviews, a designer asked me if I could draw an ellipse. I said, "Sure." He gave me a compass, a mechanical drafting pencil, and a scale. He took me to a separate room with a drafting table with a piece of paper taped to it and told me to sit down and draw a two-inch by four-inch ellipse.

At one of the next interviews, a mechanical engineer asked me if I could read a Vernier scale. Again, I said, "Sure," because, obviously, I hadn't learned my lesson at the first interview. The engineer pulled a set of calipers out of his drawer, opened it about a half-inch, and asked me to read the scale. The exact measurement was .532 inches.

Each interview got progressively more and more in-depth and complicated. I met with a couple more engineers and at least one physicist. No one asked me where I thought I could see myself in five years. No one asked me what my strengths and weaknesses were. All the questions were technical in nature.

The last interview of the day was with the man who would become my husband. I was dressed in my interview finest, a navy blue dress suit and pumps. Alan wore jeans with the knees torn out and an old polo shirt. I thought to myself, "Who is this? Why is this bum interviewing me?" Then he started asking me questions.

He said, "I see here on your resume that you've taken some Fortran classes. Would you go up to the whiteboard and write me a short program to show how you would sort something?"

By that time, I didn't even want the job. I get this red mark on my neck whenever I get upset with someone, and it was flaming. Who was this guy asking me this kind of question? I was thinking to myself, "I don't need Fortran to do a designer's job. You can shove that Fortran up your you-know-what!"

Despite having the most terrible headache because I hadn't eaten all day, I wrote the program, and I got the job.

The campus covered almost 200 acres, and the staff was spread out in many different buildings. The management came up with an Employee Activities Group as a way to bring people together. The group provided an avenue where people from the lab could meet up with others at the lab who had similar interests. There were sports groups like golf, bowling, and softball. Someone even started a genealogy club. I decided I was going to start a dog training club.

For the first year, my club was not allowed to meet in any of the lab buildings because the man who ran Facilities Management didn't want dogs in any of them. He thought the dogs would mess up the carpets. One of the initial members of our group knew the owner of the RV sales company across the street from the lab. He allowed us to meet in one of his fenced-in lots. We met once a week after work. In that first year, we trained eight dogs to become therapy dogs through Therapy Dogs International.

As word got around, more employees wanted to train their dogs but didn't want to go outside across the street. We would have to cancel every time it rained. The dogs had to perform their sits and downs on the pavement. It was okay, but not ideal. One of the administrative assistants to the CEO of the lab decided she wanted to train her golden retriever. She asked if we could use one of the state-owned buildings. It was the oldest building onsite and had a lobby about thirty feet by forty feet, approximately the same size as an obedience dog ring. The CEO agreed, overruled the facilities manager, and allowed us to meet there.

I started each class with something I called doga, dog yoga. It was a way to tell the dogs that class was starting and only took a few minutes to do. I asked the handlers to put their hands on their dogs' hearts and take three deep breaths. I counted to ten while they did so. Then I walked them through a massage for their dogs. Starting at their heads, I told them to rub the dog's ears, go down the sides of the face, and rub their jaws. Then I instructed them to take the dog by the scruff of the neck like a mama dog would do to a puppy and gently shake it. From there, with two fingers, they traveled down the dog's spine to the end of the tail. Again, I asked them to start at the head and massage the spine with two fingers, but at the shoulder blades I told them to detour down each front leg. I had them repeat this for the back legs and spend a little time rubbing the knee joints of the back legs. The dogs relaxed after this massage and focused on their handlers for the class. It was also a way to check for lumps and bumps that may not have been otherwise noticed.

One afternoon, the facilities manager who had been so against our dog training group called me.

"We have this problem with the Canada geese on the site," he said. "They poop all over the sidewalks, people track it into the buildings, and it's ruining the carpets. It's also slippery on the sidewalks, and I'm afraid someone is going to fall. I'm paying the landscaping company to hose it off the sidewalks, but it's a never-ending task. Do you think you could bring some of the dogs from the dog club to chase them away?"

I was surprised by the phone call because it was such an about-face. Usually, he called me with complaints about the dog club.

"I'm not sure that's such a good idea," I said. "I think you need a certain breed of dog like a border collie or an Australian shepherd to do that kind of work, and we don't have anyone like that in our dog club right now. I'm afraid one of the other dogs might not just chase them away but might kill them. And that wouldn't look good for our dog club. Let me think about it, and I'll get back to you."

I knew that other companies had a similar problem, so I looked up some options on the internet. I found a company that made black plastic silhouettes of border collies on springs. The landscaping company could place them around the buildings and move them every time they mowed so they weren't in the same place every time. They were an inexpensive solution to the problem.

The first night the plastic dogs were in place, an employee who showed up early for work before the sun came up pulled into the parking lot but stayed in her car. She called the guard at the front desk.

"There is a coyote by the back door, and I'm afraid to get out of my car," she said. "I can see its glowing eyes."

The plastic dogs had small round reflectors where their eyes should be. She felt foolish when the guard explained that they were scarecrow dogs.

And this wasn't the last time I got a chuckle from the plastic dogs. Every time the lab had an open house, I volunteered to ride on the buses that took people around the site. I gave a little spiel about the mission of the lab, explained what people could see at each bus stop, and answered questions. At the end of the bus ride, as people were leaving the lab, I would ask them what their favorite or most interesting part of the day was.

One woman said, "Those plastic dogs to keep the geese away are genius!"

We probe the nucleus of the atom, and she was impressed with a plastic dog.

For ten years we had a Jefferson Lab Dog Training Club, and although Sammy couldn't chase geese successfully, he was one of the stars. Every year, we would hold a class in the spring for the dogs to train for the Canine Good Citizen test and the Therapy Dog International test. Over forty dogs went on to be therapy dogs in hospitals, nursing homes, and libraries.

Chapter 18

PG Arrives

With Radar gone, and although I did appreciate spending focused time on Sammy's dancing, I didn't enjoy having just one dog. It wasn't long before I contacted James River Greyhounds and asked for another.

They had an eighteen-month-old brindle female arriving on the next haul. She had been named PG Hairspray at the track. The kennel name was PG—probably the initials of the kennel owner. They named all the dogs in PG's litter after PG movies: PG Inkheart, PG Top Gun, PG Home Alone. I kept the beginning part of her name and just called her PG. I suppose I could have renamed her Tracy after the major character in the movie *Hairspray*. But PG didn't look like a heavyset, sixteen-year-old high school student. Many people who met PG mistakenly called her PJ. My mother-in-law always called her Peaches, even when I corrected her.

When the dogs arrived from Florida on the hauler truck, the driver of the truck dropped them off at Crittertown Bath House, a pet washing facility with half a dozen bathtubs elevated a few feet off the floor. A slew of James River

Greyhound volunteers met the truck. The volunteers gave the dogs food and water. Then potential adopters were paired with a volunteer and gave their dogs a bath.

Suzanne helped me with PG. "She's a beautiful girl," she said as we lifted her gently into the tub. "I just love the brindles."

We scrubbed her from nose to tail. She shivered in the tub, and her teeth chattered. When we finished, I rubbed her all over with a big fluffy towel. She got her nails trimmed by one volunteer, and then I took her home.

She became the Robin to Sammy's Batman, the Tonto to Sammy's Lone Ranger. She was always by his side but never stole his spotlight.

One day I saw a sign in the library for a Listening Ears program at a local elementary school. It wasn't dog dancing, but I thought it might be something PG would enjoy. Listening Ears wanted people to bring their dogs to the school once a week for the children to read to them. I signed us up for it.

We arrived at the old brick school building in the afternoon. I took PG through the double blue doors with an arched transom on top.

"We're here for the Listening Ears program," I said to the secretary in the front office.

"Come with me," she said. She led me to two desks in the hallway placed in front of one of the classrooms. I positioned PG's pink fluffy dog bed next to the desks.

"The children earn privileges to read to the dogs. They'll each have an index card with the time they are allowed to read written on it. When their time is up, you send them back into the classroom and the next child will come out," she explained.

Soon a little girl in a teal blue hoodie and jeans came out of the heavy classroom door carrying a picture book. She sat at the desk next to me and opened her book. Shyly, she began reading. She stopped at every page and showed the illustration to PG.

"Your time is up," I said when she finished the book.

"Thank you for letting me read to you, PG," she said as she petted her head. She skipped back into the classroom.

The next reader was a young boy with a chapter book.

"What chapter should I read?" he asked me.

"I think you should just read from where you last left off," I said.

"But how will she know what is going on if I don't start from the beginning?" he asked.

"Good point," I said. "While you're petting her, you can tell her the beginning of the story. Then read the chapter you're on."

PG whined and play-snapped at the air when the boy left and returned to the classroom. She wanted another story!

Not only did she like reading, but PG was also my huntress. When we walked, I felt like she was saying to me, "Mommy, you are the worst squirrel hunter ever!! I'm being all stealthy and trying to sneak up on them, and you're plodding along like Godzilla making all kinds of noise! We'll never catch one!"

One morning, while walking her in the neighborhood, she made a quick bolt behind a garbage can. She snatched up a rat, shook it one time, snapped its back, and dropped it to the ground. She looked at me proudly with what I can only describe as a smile on her face and walked on as if nothing had happened.

One afternoon, I got a call at work from our dog walker. "You won't believe what PG did!"

I was used to hearing about Sammy's antics, but PG was usually much more reserved.

"I am absolutely traumatized. She caught a baby bird and brought it into the house! I told her to drop it, and she did. But the poor little thing's wing was broken," she explained. "I took it outside and put it in the grass. Do you think the mother will come back for it?"

"Oh, I don't know. I doubt it," I said. My dog walker was so empathetic with all animals, but I didn't want her to have false hope. When I got home from work, I went outside to look for it, but I think one of the neighborhood cats got it. I saw no trace of a baby bird.

Catching the baby bird additionally emboldened her to chase the geese who landed in our borrow-pit. Whenever one got close to the fence PG would run after it until it flapped its wings and took off into the sky.

PG was also a digger. One had to be careful while walking in our backyard not to twist an ankle in one of her holes. Perhaps the baby bird found its way into one of them.

Although she was a great huntress, PG reverted to a cowering, quivering mess on the Fourth of July and New Year's Eve. Fireworks, thunder, and gunshots petrified her. At the first boom, she had a routine where she paced, panted, drooled, and made herself into a small ball in a corner. Then she repeated the routine over and over again. I tried many counter-conditioning steps. I played music with thunderstorms in the background on low volume and gave her treats at every boom. I bought her a ThunderShirt, a body wrap that provided constant pressure as a calming effect. I acted like the noises were no big deal to see if she would follow my lead. I even tried a couple of different calming herbs and then eventually tranquilizers from the vet.

Once the fear took hold, she refused any attempts from me to help her. I grew to dread those holidays. I was probably the only person who prayed for rain every Fourth of July and New Year's Eve so the officials would cancel the fireworks.

Sammy, PG, and I also liked to be outside, and we walked almost every weekend at Sandy Bottom Nature Park in Hampton. The park has eleven trails and two lakes, Sandy Bottom Lake and Crystal Lake. There was one spot where the trail ran along the lake with an inclined, sandy beach-like area. On the hottest days, the dogs would wade into the water, and minnows would swarm around them. Sammy would jump like he was on a trampoline and splash down with all four legs into the water. He would stick his head under the water and blow bubbles. Then he would get back up on the solid ground, shake all over, and splatter me with water. He seemed to laugh with glee at his own stunts. PG was more delicate and tried to step on *top* of the water.

When Sammy walked on the trails, he looked back at me and joyfully barked like he was telling me something. Maybe he was saying, "Look at the beautiful leaves on that tree," or "Did you see that squirrel?" I would say, "I know, right?"

I wrote a blog for a couple of years called *Pawstcards from Hampton Roads*. I wanted to share our walking adventures with others who had similar interests. Whenever I travel, I love sending postcards back home, and I love receiving postcards. This blog was a way to share those things. I ended each post with "Wish you were here!"

I had always had black hounds, so I pleasantly accepted the compliments I got with my brindle greyhound. Her coat was reddish-brown with streaks of black. As I walked her through Gosnold's Hope Park in Hampton one day, someone yelled out of a car window, "Hey, lady, is that a tiger?"

"Yes, she is a tiger. And I have trained her to walk casually beside me on a fuchsia leash with golden dragonflies on it. It happens every day, so move over Siegfried and Roy," I replied out loud to myself as the car had already moved on.

But I also got some crazy questions. One day, when I was walking her at the beach, someone said, "Can that dog run faster than a crackhead?" I didn't know how to answer that one.

Chapter 19

Coax me

As I said earlier, when I first met my husband, Alan, I didn't like him. It was complicated. He is very clever and has a great sense of humor, but he's also arrogant, logic-obsessed, and self-centered. As we began to work together, I admired the fact that he didn't suffer fools. But if he knew that you were being mistreated, he would leap to your defense. I grew to respect how much he knew about the magnets and cryogenic systems we designed. Some of these things I had never even heard about until I worked at the lab.

When we first met, we were both married to other people. I had been married to my husband Dale for ten years and he to his wife Barb for twelve when we both got divorced.

It was around Valentine's Day when he made his feelings known to me. One of the other designers at the lab brought some heart-shaped lollipops to work. It was common for people to bring leftover birthday cake, a few extra bagels, Halloween or Christmas candy and leave it in the break room. This man's wife bought lollipops for her children to hand out at school. But some of the lollipops had inappropriate sayings on them, and she told her husband to take them to work with him. Instead of putting them in the break room, he left a lollipop on each person's desk in the design area.

All the engineering and design staff were in a series of construction trailers that were connected and called Trailer City. Beige walls, sandy-colored cubicle separators, and gray carpet surrounded the cubicle where I worked, but Alan worked in an office with a door. On each of our dreary desks was a bright red, heart-shaped lollipop with "Coax Me" in white letters.

Because I was in the trailer with the cubicles, I could see that everyone got one of these lollipops, but Alan was in his office by himself.

He sent me an email with no subject matter and only one sentence in it.

Consider yourself coaxed.

I had no idea what he was talking about. I replied with an email with just a series of question marks.

????

He sent me another email.

Didn't you leave this heart-shaped sucker on my desk?

I replied that everyone in the design group had one of those suckers on their desks.

When I saw him later in the day to discuss a design problem, we laughed about it. But the ice was broken, and we both realized there was an attraction.

We planned our first date. There was a bar called the Captain's Rail close to the lab, and we decided to meet there on a Friday evening for drinks.

Friday turned out to be a gloomy, rainy day in the middle of February. Wednesday of that week had been Valentine's

Day, and the bar seemed to be very busy with Valentine's Day couples. Instead of going inside, Alan slid into the passenger seat of my car. We kissed for the first time.

He looked at me and said, "It feels so good to have some passion in my life again." And I was captivated by him.

Once we became a couple, he was completely devoted to me. Together, we moved into a rented house at Buckroe Beach. We alternated visitation weekends with our ex-spouses. One weekend we had four kids, one weekend we had zero kids, and the weeks in the middle we had my two kids. Alan had two children, Eric and Kelly. I had two children, Eric and Jade. So we ended up with two boys both named Eric which was a little confusing at times. Jade had always called her brother, Bubba, so we all started calling him that to differentiate. On the weekends that we had zero kids, we were free to travel, to go to museums, or to go out to eat at higher-end restaurants.

Alan has an obsessive personality, and at the beginning of our relationship when I was the object of his obsession, I quite enjoyed it. He did everything that I wanted to do. We went to art museums, took art classes together, and ate dinners with wine pairings.

But soon after we got together, he bought a boat. I was no longer the obsession; the cabin cruiser was. He spent most of his spare time working on the boat. At first, he kept the boat in our backyard and worked on it there. The whole deck had to be replaced among other things. Once it was sea-worthy, he transported it to the local marina and kept it there.

One weekend, I took all four kids to Buckroe Beach. I was contentedly sitting on a blanket reading. The boys were splashing around in the surf, and the girls were playing in the sand. I had packed a cooler of sandwiches and drinks for us.

Alan strode across the sand to where we were sitting.

"I can take you on the boat to a better beach than this," he said.

"Well, we're okay here. We have a great spot, and the kids are having fun."

"They'll have so much more fun at this private beach. Please?" he asked.

I sighed, and reluctantly dried off the kids, wiped sand off them, folded up the blanket, and dragged the cooler back to the car. We followed him in his car to the marina and waited for the staff at the marina to put the boat in the water. Soon we were chugging away in the boat to this so-called private beach.

It was not so private! There were lines of boats anchored along the beach like the parking lot at Walmart. The kids had a small space of sand and water about the size of our smallest bedroom to play in. When they would venture out past where the boat was moored, I was terrified that they would get run over by people zipping by on jet skis.

"You thought this was better than where we were at the beach?" I asked him.

I began to resent having to watch his children on the weekends that he was supposed to be spending time with them, but he wanted to go out on the boat and fish.

As he prepared to go out on an excursion one weekend, I told him that he had to take his kids with him. That was the whole point of visitation weekends, to spend time with the kids.

"Can Eric and Jade come along too?" He asked.

"I'm not letting my kids go out on that boat. I don't trust it," I said.

My fears were confirmed when he and his kids didn't return that evening. At one o'clock in the morning, I received a call from the Coast Guard.

"We just want to inform you, ma'am, that your husband and kids are stranded in the Chesapeake Bay. They are safe, but they have to be towed back to the marina by a towboat."

When they finally arrived back at the marina around 3:00 a.m., the towboat launched Alan's boat into the dock and put a hole in the bow. It wasn't long after that when the boat was donated to Goodwill as a charitable contribution. He couldn't get enough by selling it to cover the money he had put into it.

After the boat, there were fixations on bowling, photography, golf, and wine. He went all-in for a year or two, and then he moved on to the next thing. I knew Alan loved me, but I never became the number one obsession again. Maybe it was just as well that he wasn't preoccupied with me. While he was bowling or golfing, I was dog training and working with the rescue group.

Alan liked most of our greyhounds, but he didn't love them the way that I did. And he couldn't stand Sammy's barking. Sammy had learned to use barking to his benefit. He never wanted to be farther than a few feet away from me. If we took him along to a restaurant with an outdoor patio to eat dinner and I got up from the table to go to the restroom, he would be so frustrated that he couldn't get to me, he would bark like a broken record. No matter what Alan said or did, he would not quiet down, and all the other restaurant patrons would stare. It was worse than having a child throwing a temper tantrum. When I returned, he would have a friendly greeting bark. I would scratch his head and say something sweet to him, inadvertently rewarding him for the barking, so the pattern continued. He would then happily and quietly settle on his blanket under the table.

I always walked the dogs first thing in the morning when I woke up at 5:30 a.m. so they could be exercised before I went to work. I tried to be quiet so I wouldn't wake Alan when I was changing into my sweatsuit, but as soon as I picked up a leash, Sammy would start to bark and spin in circles to get me to move faster. Alan would growl to himself and pull the pillow over his head. Alan probably preferred to be awakened by the smell of Sumatran coffee rather than a dog barking.

But the worst part of Sammy's barking was when I trained him to bark "I love you" to me.

"Ruh Rove Roo," he barked, just like the Jetson's dog Astro, when I prompted him.

I believe Alan was jealous of my little dog.

Chapter 20

Beach Bound Hounds

When I had established Sammy as an excellent dog dancing partner, we went to a greyhound event in Myrtle Beach, South Carolina called Beach Bound Hounds. Beach Bound Hounds was a greyhound owner's holiday at the Sea Mist Resort in September, when it was still warm enough to go to the beach but most of the summer beachgoers had gone home. The Sea Mist opened its Sandcastle Hotel right on the beach to the hounds for a four-day weekend. Beach Bound Hounds was the biggest fundraiser for Greyhounds Crossroads, a greyhound adoption group in the Carolinas and Georgia. Each year there was a different theme, and a king and queen greyhound were crowned. I was hoping to show off Sammy's dancing skills at one of the events.

The first year that we attended, the organizers arranged for us to take our dogs along with us to a local supper club that had impersonators who sang during dinner. We had a simple spaghetti and salad dinner, but the real treat was being up close and personal to the performers. The show was a variety show with "Dean Martin" as the host. "Phyllis Diller" was there with a short comedy routine. And then "Sammy Davis, Jr." came on to sing "Candy Man."

"Look at all these wonderful dogs out here this evening," Sammy said. "What are some of their names?"

"This is Sammy Davis, Jr. He's named after you," I said with an ear-to-ear smile. We were seated at one of the tables right beside the red-carpeted stage. "And he dances!"

"He dances?" Sammy questioned. "Bring him on up here!"

I took Sammy up onto the red-carpeted stage. The bright spotlights hit Sammy, and his tail was wagging a mile a minute!

Sammy did a couple of spins, and he did a figure eight around my legs. Would he do any of his more complicated dance moves? No. But what he did was enough. It was a friendly, sympathetic audience of other greyhound owners. They all broke into applause.

When we went back to our stage-side table to sit down, of course he wanted to bark! I brought along a couple of rubber dog toys with a cavity filled with peanut butter, and I kept shoving those into his mouth to keep him quiet so the show could continue.

I got some photos of Sammy Davis, Jr. with "Sammy Davis, Jr." before we left.

During the day, we could choose different fun workshops and crafts—all greyhound related. In the morning they had some contests, and PG won for the Baldest Monkey Butt. She had no fur at all on her backside, something called Bald Thigh Syndrome. Some racing greyhounds have more hair loss than others.

The organizers also coordinated a "greyhound stroll" meet and greet at an outdoor shopping venue called Barefoot

Landing. Alan and I loaded Sammy and PG into the van, and we looked forward to a fun afternoon going souvenir shopping. The dogs were allowed into certain stores. We arrived at the shopping center, and I parked. Another van with a load of kids parked right next to us. The kids distracted me as I was getting the dogs out of the van, and I accidentally shut the van door on the last six inches of Sammy's beautiful long tail. He screamed the greyhound scream of death. The end of his tail was hanging loosely, and there was a lot of blood. This was a lot worse than happy tail.

I was just heartsick that I had done such a thing. How quickly an afternoon went from laughing and having a good time to a nightmare. We looked for a first aid station in the shopping area and stumbled upon the information center.

"Do you have a first aid kit?" I frantically asked the woman at the desk. I had Sammy on a leash beside me with his tail dripping blood on the floor.

I didn't even want to say it. "I shut my dog's tail in the van door, and it's bleeding."

Her look filled me with guilt. "Oh, dear. We have a small first aid kit over there on the wall."

Unfortunately, it had little to bandage up a dog's tail. The kit had a couple of packs of Tylenol, alcohol wipes, some tweezers, and a few individual packs of antibiotic ointment. They had some band-aids which I tried to piece together around his tail.

Since we were on vacation, I didn't know any of the local vets. We returned to the hotel, and I looked in the Beach Bound Hounds brochure for the on-call vet. She met us in her room back at the Sandcastle Hotel. The vet wrapped his tail in neon-green vet wrap and gave me some painkillers for him.

She advised me to have the tail amputated when we returned to Hampton from our vacation. She said it was going to die and fall off if I did nothing because no blood was flowing to the end of the tail anymore.

That put a damper on the rest of the weekend. I didn't want to take him to the beach because I didn't want to get sand in his cut. We had one more group dinner to attend, along with a silent auction. Everyone had heard about the woman who shut her dog's tail in the car door. I thought people were whispering about me and staring at my poor dog. I felt bad enough without having to answer all the questions about what happened.

We went to the dinner and then went back to our hotel room for the last evening. Believe it or not, we won a big barrel of cheese popcorn in the silent auction. I was lying on the bed in the hotel eating some of it.

Both Sammy and PG looked at me like, "I, too, would like some cheese popcorn."

Sammy ate his. I guess the painkillers that he was on numbed his broken tail enough that he was interested in eating food.

But like a two-year-old, PG proceeded to lick the cheese off and left soggy popcorn all over the bedspread for me to pick up.

Before we left, I looked out the window of our room and saw dozens of hounds and their owners out on the beach for the Sunrise Walk. I said to Sammy and PG, "If your mother wasn't so careless, you'd be down there right now." They looked up from their cozy place on the bed and didn't seem to mind that they weren't down on the beach.

Although this was accidental, it reminded me of a neglectful incident I had with my mother, not on a warm sunny beach day in South Carolina but a cold winter evening in Pennsylvania.

In sixth grade, my teacher picked me to take part in our elementary school's spelling bee. I was an avid reader and could spell many words above my grade level. Getting selected for the spelling bee gave me some angst because they held the practices after school. That meant someone would have to come to the school to pick me up.

After the first practice, my dad picked me up, and there was no problem. But after the second practice, my mom was supposed to pick me up. I stood outside the school, peering through the chain-link fence, and she was nowhere to be seen. All the other kids had left with their parents. It started to get dark.

The teacher who ran the spelling bee came out of the school. "Your mom's not here yet?" he asked.

"She'll be here," I said. I pulled my knit hat down closer on my head and then crossed my arms over my chest.

"Maybe I should give you a ride home," he said.

This caused me to panic. In my head I was thinking, "If I ride home with him and my mom shows up, she'll be furious with me for leaving. But if I don't ride home with him and she doesn't show up, I'll have to walk home from the school for several miles in the dark."

"No, she'll be here. I don't need a ride," I said to him, choosing what I thought was the better choice.

"It's getting dark. I'll wait with you till she gets here," he said. He was wearing just his suit jacket without a coat, and his tie was fluttering in the wind.

Now there was more trepidation. If she showed up drunk, she would be seething if she thought I asked him to wait with me, although I didn't ask him. And if she showed up drunk, I wasn't sure what my teacher would do. Would he allow me to get in the car with her?

"You don't have to wait. I'll be fine," I said as lightheartedly as I could muster. He ignored me and continued to stand beside me.

In a few minutes, we saw headlights coming down the street toward the school. It was her Oldsmobile Delta 88 convertible.

She didn't get out of the car but just leaned over and rolled down the passenger-side window.

"Thank you for waiting with her," she slurred to my teacher. "Get in," she said to me. I could smell the alcohol along with the Chanel No. 5 perfume she wore.

"No problem," my teacher said. I guess he was cold and wanted to get home himself.

I sat quietly for the ride home. The next night at practice, my dad was supposed to pick me up. On purpose, I spelled "handkerchief" wrong. I left out the "d." That eliminated me from further practice.

"This is my last practice. I don't have to go back," I said to my dad.

"Why?"

"I spelled a word wrong, and no one else did," I said.

"What word did you spell wrong?" he asked.

"I missed the 'd' in handkerchief," I said.

He laughed at me.

That irrational feeling came back to me when I thought all the other hound owners were talking about the woman who shut her dog's tail in the van door. The spotlight was on me again, but not in a good way.

Chapter 21

Things Gifted To Me

A pair of size eleven black Toms shoes with a white greyhound screen printed on them and a pair of size eleven red Toms shoes with a turquoise greyhound screen printed on them

A wooden puzzle in the shape of a greyhound that spells the word "Greyhound"

A bedside lamp with greyhounds stenciled on the lampshade

A fleece blanket with a greyhound's face printed on it in kaleidoscope fashion

Bracelets, earrings, and necklaces with greyhound charms

A life-size concrete greyhound garden statue

Canvas tote bags with greyhounds screen printed on them

A greyhound beach towel

A purse-sized notebook that says "Keep Calm and Adopt a Greyhound"

A two-foot-tall white ceramic statue of a sitting greyhound

A six-inch-tall black statue of a sitting greyhound made from the horn of an African goat

A papier-mâché greyhound

A bobble-head greyhound
Socks with greyhounds on them
A set of wine glasses with standing greyhounds etched on them
A return address stamp in the shape of a greyhound
A t-shirt with greyhounds on it that says, "We Don't Ride in Purses"

Chapter 22

A Little White Wedding Chapel

For our tenth wedding anniversary in 2006, Alan and I went to Las Vegas and renewed our wedding vows. This was a second marriage for both of us. We thought that reaffirming our commitment to each other might help us to skip the rough periods that occurred in our first marriages at around the ten-year mark. Sammy and PG were boarded, and we flew to Las Vegas.

We found a package deal for a Las Vegas wedding. It included a limousine ride from our hotel, champagne in the limo, a bouquet of roses for me, a boutonniere for Alan, and a ceremony at A Little White Wedding Chapel. A Little White Wedding Chapel was known for many celebrity weddings, but one that stood out for us was Britney Spears's quick marriage to her childhood friend, which was then annulled a few days later.

I bought a light cream-colored suit with a lacey blouse. We stayed at the Bellagio Hotel and Casino, so I went to their spa during the day for a manicure, pedicure, hair, and makeup. Both Alan and I were excited and thought this was going to be fun.

The limo pulled up to the small white chapel surrounded by a white-painted, iron fence with an open-heart design on top of each fence post. There was a lightbox sign atop a tall pole with the name of the chapel and "Joan Collins and Michael Jordan were married here." Although not to each other. There was also a twenty-four-hour drive-up wedding window advertised as a Drive-Thru Tunnel of Love.

When we arrived inside the chapel, we had a choice of getting married by an Elvis impersonator or a regular minister. The couple before us had chosen Elvis, so we thought we would give Elvis a break and go with the regular minister. He was a great Elvis impersonator but nowhere near as good as the Sammy Davis, Jr. impersonator we met at Beach Bound Hounds. Everyone was laughing and having a good time. We walked to the front of the chapel where the older, female minister was standing. Behind her stood a white cupid statue holding a huge bouquet of colored flowers above his head. To the left, a light shined through a stained-glass window of two doves in a heart. On the wall behind the cupid statue, a swath of some golden trompe l'oeil draperies adorned the pink-and-white-flower-patterned wallpaper.

We grinned foolishly at each other as the minister began to speak.

"Today we welcome Alan and Joyce as they celebrate their love and renew the promises they made to each other on their wedding day ten years ago," she said to an empty room of white pews. I glanced around the room, still smiling at the absurdity of it all.

Then she began speaking directly to us.

"You've been married for ten years, so you've had some good times and some bad times. But the fact that you're here today means that there were more good times than bad. Please join hands," she said.

"Joyce, will you continue to have Alan as your husband and continue to live in this marriage?" she asked me.

"I will," I answered.

"Do you reaffirm your love for him, and will you love, honor, and cherish him in sickness and in health, for richer or poorer, for better or worse, forsaking all others as long as you both shall live?"

"I do," I said as I looked over at Alan. Tears began to well in my eyes. Suddenly, the whole ceremony didn't feel like fun and games anymore. We were rekindling the old feelings.

When Alan saw me start to cry, then he started to cry, too. He could barely get through his part of the vows.

"Alan and Joyce, in remembrance of this day, as a reaffirmation of your love and of the vows you have spoken here today, please give each other a single red rose each year on your anniversary. In the best of marriages, there are difficult times. There are times of hurtful words, times of neglect, times when we must wait patiently to be together again. Those may be times when the words you need to speak are difficult. I ask that you remember this moment and that when words fail you, that you place a single rose on your spouse's pillow as a way to say, 'I remember our vow' and 'I love you.' Let this exchanging of roses be the beginning of a lifelong tradition of unspoken love."

We were both sobbing.

"It is with pleasure that I conclude this ceremony of renewing the vows of marriage that joined you and binds you as husband and wife. Please celebrate with a kiss!" she said as she closed her book. We were still sniffling a little as we kissed.

As we rode back to the Bellagio in the limousine, I stared out the window at the lights on the Strip while remembering our actual wedding day.

We chose February 16 as the date for our wedding because it was the anniversary of our first date at the Captain's Rail. We planned to get married at a small restaurant, Fire and Ice. Because it was a second wedding for both of us, we wanted just a small, intimate ceremony. Alan's parents and his brother came from Michigan. Alan's brother was his best man, and one of my girlfriends came from Pennsylvania to be my matron of honor. One woman who worked with us at Jefferson Lab came with her husband. Our four children completed the guest list.

It started snowing in the morning. By the time of the wedding at 6:00 p.m., there were about ten inches of snow on the ground. In the south, everything shuts down when it snows like that. The region is not equipped to handle snow removal. I called the restaurant and asked if they were going to stay open.

"If you're coming with your wedding party, we're staying open," the owner said.

The minister was the first to cancel because he was afraid to drive in the snow. I couldn't blame him as I don't like to drive in the snow either. For that matter, I don't like snow at all.

"If one of my friends comes and picks you up and takes you back home, will you come?" I asked him over the phone. He agreed.

One of the good things was that as a result of the bad weather, we had the whole restaurant to ourselves. We played some tinny-sounding wedding music on a boom box. The minister performed the ceremony, and we all sat down to eat dinner afterward. The minister chose to be driven home rather than stay to eat.

Instead of the usual white wedding cake, I asked the pastry chef at the restaurant to make us a chocolate cheesecake for the wedding cake. Alan's mother brought along these two rare, celluloid, bride-and-groom kewpie dolls, which had been on every one of their family wedding cakes for generations.

"I really don't want those dolls on my wedding cake," I said to Alan. "They were on the cake at your first wedding. I think they still even have the frosting on their feet from that cake. And they're just creepy."

"My grandparents won them at a carnival stand at Coney Island. They were on my parents' cake. They've been on every wedding cake in my family. My aunt even made clothes for them that match your dress and my suit," he argued.

"All right, we can use the dolls," I reluctantly agreed.

When it was time to cut the cake, we removed the dolls from the top and laid them on the table. As Alan and I began to cut through the cake, both of our hands pushing down on the knife, we caused the table to tilt. The bride doll rolled in what seemed to me like slow motion across the table and fell on the tile floor with a loud *crack*. Her legs and torso were in two separate parts on the floor.

Alan's mother gasped.

"It's a clean break," Alan said as he lifted the bride doll from the floor.

"It was an accident. I didn't do that on purpose. I'll get her fixed. I'll find a dollmaker that can repair her," I rambled on. I hoped that the combination of the snow and the bride doll breaking wasn't an omen of bad things to come in the future.

Alan brought my attention back to the limousine driving down the Las Vegas Strip when he popped open the champagne. We clinked glasses as we made our usual toast.

"To us and those like us," Alan said.

"Damn few of us left," I replied.

Back at the Bellagio, we walked past the breathtaking Bellagio fountains and had dinner in Michael Mina's restaurant. No snow on this day, just a view of the Conservatory and Botanical Gardens. They had a special display for Lunar New Year. It was a magical night.

I loved my husband. I had just promised at our vow renewal to love him for better or worse, in sickness and in health. But I didn't know at the time that it would be the last night of real intimacy for us due to his problems with his disease. And as much as I loved my husband, I could hardly wait to get home to Sammy and PG.

Chapter 23

Grapehounds

As I loved to travel to any greyhound events with Sammy, one of my favorites was the Grapehound Wine Tour. The original wine tour was held at Seneca Lake, New York in July, and it grew to become a celebration of not only wine tasting but also greyhound adoption. The event was a way for greyhound adopters to relax, enjoy the wine-tasting area, and relish their hounds. Several hundred adopters and their hounds attended. It was a sight to see dozens of greyhounds and their owners spread out on colorful blankets in front of the grapevines at the various vineyards, creating an eye-catching patchwork quilt spread by a giant hand.

In 2010, the organizers expanded the tour to include some wineries in Leesburg, Virginia. Their first event was on Mother's Day weekend. Wine and greyhounds make me happy, so I immediately signed up with Sammy in tow. I initially hoped that Sammy and I could do a dog dancing demonstration for the attendees, but I also thought that it was a perfect way for me to spend Mother's Day with my fur kids.

Gazing over the vineyards and little wine-tasting rooms also took me back to the boat trip through the south of France with Pascal and Helene. With each glass of wine, I remembered all our talks about how I would find the perfect dog one day. And here a sea of greyhounds surrounded me.

Northgate Estate Vineyard held the opening event on Friday evening. A food truck was serving BBQ. The greyhounds spread out across the grounds next to the vines, some with their noses in the air to sniff that smell of charred meat on the grill. I found a table for us on the patio with Sammy and PG on their blanket underneath it. It wasn't long before a female hound from the next table made her way to our blanket and squeezed in between them.

I left the dogs at the table and approached the tent where the wine tasting was taking place. When we registered, the organizers had given us tickets for wine tastings at several wineries.

"Do you like whites or reds?" the server asked me.

"I like them both," I replied.

"I want you to try this. It's called Rkatsiteli, a wine made from white grapes that originated in the country of Georgia. It is one of the oldest wine varieties in the world. It grows well in Virginia's warmer climate, and we're one of the few wineries who make it," she said as she splashed some white wine into my Grapehounds stemless glass.

"I want an entire bottle of it," I said as soon as I sipped it.

I spent the rest of the evening sipping my Rkatsiteli, eating from my cheese plate, and looking at all the greyhound ears. Some sported the neatly folded tucked ears. Others looked like bat wings. Occasionally, I would see one with one ear folded backward and one forward. Sammy's ears stood straight up at attention.

The next day we went to Lost Creek Winery, and Alan joined us. The tasting room was already full of greyhounds when we got there. Sammy and PG leaned against me at the bar. The grandfather of the couple who owned the winery was the server for our tasting.

Cabernet Sauvignon does not grow very well in Virginia, but we sipped the wines he poured for us. Any Paris sommelier will tell you that it is more distinguished to sip and spit because it allows you to better assess the flavors of the wine. My husband is a spitter. He just gets the taste in his mouth and then spits it into a container rather than swallows. One can taste a lot of wine with this method without getting drunk. I am not a spitter.

For the next wine, the grandfather rinsed our glasses with water. As he was handing the glass back to my husband, he noticed that there were still a few drops of water in the bottom of it. The old man quickly took the glass back from him and shook it out.

"We don't want any water getting into your next glass of wine. That would ruin the taste," he said.

Alan and I looked at each other and politely continued the tasting. But when we were out of earshot, Alan said with a conspiratorial wink, "Water would not ruin that wine."

Some greyhounds were snoozing on the winery floor, and we gingerly stepped over them when we finished our tasting. The winery had a huge white event tent with greyhound vendors selling coats, leashes, collars for the hounds, and greyhound-themed jewelry and apparel for the humans. Sammy stuck his nose through the rainbow display of brightly colored velvet leashes and barked at whoever would listen. We walked through the tent, and a woman selling dog treats stopped us.

"Would your dog like a homemade treat? We have lots of flavors. Peanut butter. Carrot. Pumpkin."

"You can try," I said.

She held out a treat to Sammy. He took it gingerly in his mouth and then projectile spit the treat in an arc across the aisle of the vendor tent. I thought to myself it was fortunate that Alan didn't spit like that while tasting wine.

"I guess he doesn't like them," I said apologetically. Sammy just looked up at me, wagged his tail, and moved on.

On Sunday morning there was always a group hound walk. Some dogs were content to walk beside their owners. Others jockeyed for the front position just like in their race days. Most were sporting the new collars they got at the event, so the walk became a kaleidoscope of colors and textures.

One year, someone from the adoption group was a Civil War re-enactor, so he gave a brief talk at the Ball's Bluff Battlefield before we went on the walk. This reminded me again of the boat trip through France, where we capitalized on any opportunity to stop and learn some local history along with our wine drinking.

The Civil War re-enactor stood on a rock in front of the park's visitor center and said, "This was one of the first battles of the Civil War and decidedly a Confederate victory. There were 1700 men on each side, but the casualties were not even at all. On the Confederate side, thirty-eight dead, 110 wounded, and three taken prisoner. On the Union side, 223 dead, 223 wounded, and 553 taken prisoner. A young nineteen-year-old second lieutenant, Willie Grout, pushed a large piece of driftwood out into the river. He put five men on the driftwood and swam them diagonally across the Potomac River. They became a target for the Confederate soldiers. He took several rounds in the back and the last thing he said was, 'Tell the Colonel I did my best.' Then he sank below the water. His body washed up three weeks later and was found by a congressional representative and his wife walking along Hains Point in Washington, DC. That story became the subject of one of the most popular Civil War songs, 'Vacant Chair,' by George F. Root."

The Civil War re-enactor sang a few lines of the sad chorus for us. We walked on through the trees to get to the cemetery.

The speaker stood next to a hand-hewn wooden fence around the cemetery and continued his talk. "There are only twenty-six stones in the Ball's Bluff cemetery, but there were fifty-four men buried here. Only one stone has the name of a soldier on it, James Allen of the Fifteenth Massachusetts Infantry. All the other stones simply say 'Unknown.' The commander of the Union forces, Edward E. Baker, was the only US senator ever to die in combat. The most famous survivor of this battle was Oliver Wendell Holmes, Jr. who became an associate justice on the Supreme Court."

It was eerie to stand on a trail in the woods overlooking the river and think about the battle that happened that day. Even the dogs were quiet as they seemed to understand they were standing in a sacred place.

For the Sunday afternoon farewell event, the group met at Willowcroft Farm Winery in Leesburg. It was on our way home, so that was convenient, and it became my favorite winery on the tour. The winery sits atop Mount Gilead and has a beautiful view of the Blue Ridge Mountains. The tasting room was in their old red barn, and the parking lot was in a field beside it. As I was getting the dogs out of the back of the car, a six-foot-long black snake slithered past us in the grass, and I jumped. The dogs didn't seem to care as much as I did. The snake didn't deter us.

I ventured up the earthen ramp leading to two huge white barn doors and entered their tasting room with the two dogs in tow. The barn had been the home of Fitzrah, a former 1950s steeplechase champion. I found this out as the tasting room had a book by a local author on Fitzrah for sale. I thought it was fitting to end our weekend at the home of a former racer.

The server, who could pass for Captain America, put a list of wines in front of me. "You can taste up to seven wines," he said.

I pulled my Grapehounds glass out of my tote bag and picked three whites, three reds, and one dessert wine. I didn't need to taste any further when I got to the Albariño wine. It was a light-bodied white that resembled Sauvignon Blanc but had more mineral notes. I forgot all about the Rkatsiteli at Northgate. This became my new favorite.

We set up our blanket near a picnic table on the hillside and sipped our Albariño. Sammy and PG were so tired that Sammy laid his head on PG's side and used her as a pillow.

I thought I might make a dog dancing movie while at Grapehounds to capture the feeling of a weekend with my favorite things—greyhounds, dog dancing, and wine. Sammy and I did a few dance moves in front of each winery entrance, and I recorded them on a little camcorder. I made some cardboard cutouts with a painting of a dog snout and a wine glass, which I could hold in front of Sammy's face to make it look like he was tasting wine. I thought I would pull them out at Willowcroft and video some more. But as the weekend ended and the dogs were content to lounge on the blanket beside me, I was happy enough just gazing at the view.

Before we left, we raised our glasses with the following toast: "A toast to the hounds we've loved and lost."

"And to the ones yet to come."

Chapter 24

Walking the dogs

Sammy, PG, and I took advantage of a group called Around Town Hounds that walked with their hounds to different locations in Richmond on the third Sunday of each month. This walk was a way to discover beautiful places around the city of Richmond. The January walk was always to Hollywood Cemetery. Fidos After Five at Lewis Ginter Botanical Gardens was a summer destination. The First Day Hike on New Year's Day was at Pocahontas State Park. The group started with only a dozen members and then grew to almost 300. I made many friends in this group, and the greyhounds seemed to enjoy getting out together just as much as the people did. The hounds seemed comforted to know that their racing days were not the last time they would see others that looked just like them.

If dog dancing was a way to bond with just one dog, this group created a community. It was fun to see the stares of people watching such a large group of hounds all walking together.

On a Saturday morning in December, about a dozen members of the Around Town Hounds group met up at the Williamsburg Holiday Farmer's Market, and afterward, we walked down Duke of Gloucester Street, also appropriately known as DOG Street. There were lots of tourists from different countries visiting Colonial Williamsburg for the holidays.

"Is this a greyhound parade?" someone from the crowd yelled out. "Can we pet your dogs?"

It wouldn't be long before we were surrounded by a group of people who were petting the dogs and asking their names.

"I've never seen a greyhound up close before. I've seen pictures of them racing, or, you know, an image of one on the side of a bus. Do they make good pets? I would think they need a lot of exercise," asked a woman dressed in a puffy ski coat and a headband that looked like reindeer antlers.

"They make wonderful pets. They're so docile and used to being around other animals and people. They really don't need a lot of exercise. A few walks a day, and they're happy," I replied.

We would satisfy the curiosity of that group, walk another dozen steps, and be surrounded by another group of people. It reminded me again of that Aesop's Fable and that yellow lab with the mosquitoes on its face in France.

"Could we take a picture of them with one of the Colonial Williamsburg people?" a woman in the next group asked. Colonial Williamsburg had hundreds of historical interpreters dressed in colonial garb scattered in front of their buildings.

I walked up to the woman dressed in a long brown gown and a white apron covered with a heavy wool cloak.

"Would you hold the leashes of the dogs so we can get a photo?" I asked.

"Pray pardon me. What is it that you wish me to do? Won't you be needing a sketch to capture my likeness?" She wasn't breaking character.

"We'll take the photo with a camera," I said.

"Yea, and I suppose it will be all right," she said.

Sammy in his black and white checked coat and PG in her pink argyle sweater stood in front of the woman with a wreath made of pine boughs and oyster shells behind her head. It made a wonderful picture.

My favorite walk with the group was in Richmond at Christmastime along Monument Avenue to look at Christmas decorations and lights. This was the same Monument Avenue where Easter on Parade was held. We met up with the group at the Jefferson Davis Memorial, and it was dark when we arrived. They knew we were there because they could hear Sammy barking on the other side of the monument.

"Sammy's here!" someone from the group would call out, and others would echo it.

The Guinness World Record for the loudest bark belongs to a golden retriever who registered an ear-ringing 113.1 decibels. And the record for nonstop barking goes to a cocker spaniel who barked 907 times in ten minutes. I believe Sammy could have challenged both of those records!

At the corner of Monument Avenue and Strawberry Street was the "Christmas Cadillac," a white 1966 Cadillac that the owner filled with presents, stuffed animals, and mannequins. Eight flying reindeer pulled the car up into the trees lit up with Christmas lights. I always enjoyed the lit-up flamingo on the top of the car.

One sunny November morning, the group traveled to Hampton, and we walked the hounds on the beach at the Grandview Nature Preserve. There was a three-quarters of a mile path through the salt marsh to get to the natural beach on the Chesapeake Bay. At the end of the path, before one went over the dunes to the beach, the sound of the waves crashing met the group. The secluded beach had lots of tidal debris like seaweed and sponges for the dogs to sniff. They probably would have rolled in a few dead fish if given the chance. For the people, there were many interesting shells, rocks, driftwood, and sea glass to collect. Old jetties and the ruins of the Back River Lighthouse stuck out of the water. A hurricane in the 1950s destroyed the lighthouse, and just a pile of rubble at its base was still visible.

I had done a little research on the history of the lighthouse, and I told the group this story as we walked along the beach.

"There were rumors that the lighthouse was haunted by a woman named Jenny Kane. She drowned under suspicious circumstances at the lighthouse in 1931. Her husband, Elisha, a university professor, was suspected of killing her. Elisha's father was a respected surgeon who had removed his own appendix and fixed his own hernia. His grandfather was a Union army general and abolitionist. Newspapers up and down the East Coast covered the trial, but Elisha was found not guilty. At twilight, it's said that Jenny's ghost can be seen scrambling over the rocks, wearing her weighted down wool swimsuit."

The greyhounds didn't care about the ghost stories. They are funny when they get on sand. Because they race on sand, as soon as they get on the beach, they get the zoomies and want to run as fast as they can. A zoomie is an explosion of energy with frantic running in circles or spinning around. They chased the sea foam along the waves.

I took along one of my foster dogs, Homer, on this walk. Homer belonged to Gil, but Gil was going through some tough times, and I agreed to keep him for a few weeks. A few weeks turned into a few months. Homer was a special dog, and only a few people could handle him. He was a big light fawn dog with a black face. At his first home, he had a disagreement with the couple's son. Homer took the boy's t-shirt into his crate with him. When the little boy crawled into the crate to retrieve the t-shirt, Homer snapped at him. He didn't bite him, but it was too close for comfort. I couldn't fault Homer for that because the crate should have been his own safe space.

I would have loved Homer much more if he hadn't given me spit showers so often. My guess is he had some Saint Bernard in him.

We then tried to re-home him with an older couple in Richmond's Fan District. They had quite the setup for a hound. They had hollowed out the end of the island in their kitchen to be a cozy, dark dog crate. When I took Homer there for a visit, every time the man would try to attach the leash to his collar, Homer would emit this low, menacing growl. I could leash him with no problem, but others couldn't. So, just like I had done with Radar several years ago when I took him from home to home but then decided to keep him, Gil kept Homer.

While I was fostering Homer, he did many things to make my heart stop. Usually, at the end of a dog walk around our neighborhood, I brought the dogs up onto the front porch, unclipped their leads, opened the front door, and the dogs went inside. But one day after walking Homer, I unclipped their leads, my two dogs went inside the house, and Homer took off running in the other direction down the street.

Dogs love the chase game, so I knew not to run after him. One item we have for getting greyhounds' attention in this situation is a predator call. It's a ribbed, plastic tube about eight inches long. When you squeeze it, it makes the sound of an animal like a rabbit in distress. I ran inside the house and got the "squawker."

I no sooner had the squawker out on the front porch, squawking it, than Homer came tearing back down the street toward the house. He ran right up the steps and flew inside. I'm sure he was very disappointed when no dying rabbit was lying on the floor.

Radar and Homer were not the only bounceback hounds. One woman called the adoption group and said that her hound, Grady, kept escaping their house. She said he knew how to open the door and go outside. She lived near a busy four-lane road, and she was afraid he was going to get hit by a car, so she wanted to return him for his own good. Now I didn't believe that was the real reason for returning him, but I picked him up and took him back to my house.

On Monday when I returned from work, there were teeth marks on the front handle of the door! Grady had been trying to turn the doorknob and get outside. If I hadn't seen it with my own eyes, I still would not have believed he was the "Houdini" hound. He also chewed up a couple of magazines and shredded paper all over the floor because he needed something to keep his mouth busy. Grady eventually went to live with a single guy who took him camping and on hikes. It was the perfect fit for him—he needed to be outside.

We lived very close to Buckroe Beach and walked there year-round except summer. During the summer tourist time, dogs were not allowed on the beach. Sammy liked the beach and liked to pick up trash as we walked along. He would carry a plastic soda or water bottle from wherever he found it back to the trash can on the boardwalk.

As sweet as Sammy was, if there was ever a doubt that he would protect me, he proved it one day at the beach when a grizzled man with a beard wearing dirty clothes walked up behind me. I had already put the dogs in the van, and I was opening the door to get in myself.

"Hey, babe," the man snarled at me. "Do you have any change?" He startled me because I didn't know how he got so close to me so quickly. I had just put the dogs in the van, and no one was around. I jumped.

Sammy went ballistic in the van. He was barking, growling, and gnashing his teeth. He jumped from the back of the van into the drivers' seat. I grabbed him by the collar before he could get outside and attack the guy. The man backed away at full tilt. I guess greyhounds who bark can be great guard dogs.

But that encounter with the vagrant didn't stop Sammy and me from taking city trips. One weekend in May, Norfolk had the forty-foot-tall Rubber Duck on display at the inlet of the Hague where the Chrysler Museum is located. The creator of the inflated sculpture was a Dutch artist named Florentijn Hofman. As an avid art lover, I had to visit it. And of course I took the dogs along with me.

It was a very warm day. People were picnicking in the grass along the walkway to the museum. Sammy walked up to some people sitting on a blanket. I thought he was saying hello and asking to be petted. To my horror, he helped himself to a drink of the man's ice water from his glass.

"I'm so sorry," I said to the guy. "Let me buy you another bottle of water from one of the food vendors."

"It's okay," the man said. "It's boiling hot today and they're thirsty. We have more water in our cooler." And he let both Sammy and PG slurp ice water from his glass.

From seeing Sammy and PG with the other greyhounds in our Around Town Hounds group to exploring new paths just for the three of us, I enjoyed the stimulation of walking the dogs. It made me happy because I thought it made them happy, no matter where we were walking. I believe that the dogs got joy not only from the sights and sounds but also the smells of the walks. Just like the dancing, it was another way to bond with my dogs.

Chapter 25

Surprising Suffolk

Finding new places to train dogs for dog dancing always proved difficult. Not only did I have the therapy dog class at Jefferson Lab, but I also taught an additional dog dancing class every week. When my friend Pat passed away from cancer, we no longer had use of her converted garage. I had been doing the dog dancing training at a community center in Newport News, but one night when we arrived for class, there was a note on the door that said the building had been foreclosed. We went inside to find wires where there had been light fixtures hanging from the walls. The kitchen cabinets had all been removed with only paint stains on the wall to show where they had been.

One of the ladies who trained with us asked her church if we could use their parish hall, and they said yes. So I began traveling with Sammy to Suffolk once a week on Thursday evenings for a class at St. Paul's Episcopal Church.

St. Paul's Episcopal Church was a red brick building in the Gothic Revival style on Main Street in Suffolk. The church had a stained-glass window by Louis Comfort Tiffany with an image of Jesus in the temple as a boy with a lion by his knee. We didn't get to see this magnificent piece of art when we were there as we were permitted to use only the parish hall.

The choir also practiced on Thursday evenings, so the choir director would let us in. The church was large enough that we couldn't hear them singing and they couldn't hear us playing music on our boombox. We would practice for an hour and a half, sweep up any dog hair we left behind, and go home. It was an hour's drive for me to get there.

We had an amiable group of ladies and dogs. Leslie had been in my original dog dancing class at Merrimac and had Swiss mountain dogs. Vicki had an Australian shepherd. Shelly had a pit bull mix, and a Labrador retriever, and Elyse had a hound mix. We started the same way as we had in the past. We began by looking at the dog's gait and picking music for them.

Shelly developed a nice routine to "Stand By Me" for Max, and Elyse had a touching routine for Leo to "You Don't Mess Around with Jim."

I played "Puff the Magic Dragon" as a possible freestyle song for Shelly's little rescued red pitbull at class, and it was magic! Her tail started to wag, she got a little pep in her step, and it's possible she even smiled. It was one more reason I continued to love freestyle class.

"Ladies, I have an idea for a new routine for Sammy," I said to them one evening. "I want to recreate the marionette I envisioned the first time I saw him with a tennis ball between his front paws."

"That will be so cute!" Shelly said.

"I have some ideas for a prop," said Elyse, who was an artist who could whip up almost anything.

She helped me fashion a hand controller cross out of cardboard strips. I hung strings of brightly colored ribbon from the ends of the crossbar, which would control his feet. A string from the back of the main bar would control his tail and one from the front would control his head. The strings wouldn't be physically tied to him, of course, but would give the illusion of being attached.

"I'm going to wear a black and white harlequin clown costume. The song I picked for the routine is 'I'm Your Puppet' by James and Bobby Purify," I told them.

Sammy would start in a down position. I would lift the front of the hand controller as I gave him the command to rise to a sit. Then I would lift the back of the cross and command him to rise to a stand. I trained him to lift first one paw and then the other, and I could make that look like I was controlling it by swiveling the crossbar. We moved around the ring, and he circled me, or I circled him. And at the end, I did that opening routine in reverse to make it look like I was putting him back in his puppet's box by first dropping his rear end and then dropping his front. I thought this could be a prize-winning routine.

We started practicing, and the ladies also thought it was a winner.

One night, the church was locked when we got there, so I left Sammy in the van while I went to find the choir director to let us in. The choir director opened one of the side doors. Then we walked inside the church to the back door. While we were walking to the door, we could hear someone outside beeping their car horn.

The choir director said, "Someone sure is impatient!"

And when he opened the door, with me standing directly behind him, we saw it was Sammy laying on the horn!

He said, "I don't believe it! That's your DOG blowing the horn!"

As if his barking wasn't bad enough...

It was not long after we started this class in Suffolk that Sammy had his first grand mal seizure. I didn't know what was happening to him. He was lying on the couch beside me, and soon he slipped off the couch in slow motion like a melting clock in a Dali painting. Then he started twitching on the floor and drooling. Eventually, the jerking stopped, and he regained consciousness.

By the time I realized he was having a seizure, it was over. He seemed dazed and confused. It was quite frightening for me. As soon as he seemed himself again, I packed him into the car to take him to the emergency vet. One of the most worrisome things about dogs having seizures is that it raises their temperature. Greyhounds already have strong metabolisms with higher body temperatures, so that was a tremendous concern. I was worried he'd have brain damage. I cried as I drove to the vet. I couldn't bear losing Sammy.

The emergency vet took some blood, and then Sammy and I waited in the examining room for what seemed like an interminable amount of time. Finally, I asked the vet tech if I could have a blanket for him to lie down on, and the tech gave me a thin blue flannel blanket. Sammy didn't want to lie on the cold, hard tile floor. The vet found no obvious reason for Sammy to have the seizure. He suggested I wait and see if he would have another one. If so, he wanted me to keep a logbook on the duration of the seizures. If he had them often enough, he would prescribe phenobarbital for him. In the end, the diagnosis was idiopathic epilepsy, which meant that he had seizures of unknown origin.

Once Sammy started barking again, I thought he was getting better. He even barked in his sleep.

Five days later, Sammy had another seizure during the night. But if the previous seizure was a five, this one was a one. He got a dazed look on his face, rolled off the couch onto the floor, and then his legs stiffened. It lasted only a few minutes. I started to keep a diary as it looked like he was going to be doing this for a while.

I continued with his dog dancing despite his prognosis. I wanted to perfect the marionette routine.

Marilyn and I were invited to do a promotional video for the Mutt Strut, the annual fundraiser for the Suffolk Humane Society. I know they didn't pick the hottest day of the summer on purpose, but that's when the filming was scheduled. Marilyn brought her pug, Rocket, and I brought Sammy to the park field where the event was going to be held. Marilyn left Rocket in the van with the air conditioning running. I kept Sammy in the shade of a nearby shed.

"I want to practice with him a few times before the camera crew gets here," I said.

"I think it's too hot," Marilyn said. "I'm leaving Rocket in the van."

I had decided to do our old "Hit the Road, Jack" routine because the puppet routine wasn't ready. Sammy's tongue was hanging nearly to the ground after we practiced a couple of times. I should have listened to Marilyn because Sammy knew that routine by heart.

Finally, the camera crew showed up. The interviewer asked us a couple of questions. The cameraman hoisted his camera to his shoulder, and they started filming.

Sammy slowly plodded along beside me and would do none of his tricks. Luckily, Rocket was more animated and pulled off the commercial.

Summer turned to fall and then winter. A friend from work asked my Suffolk dog dancing group to do a demonstration at a winter holiday party for Refugee Resettlement in Newport News. Many of the refugees from Middle Eastern countries did not speak English but they understood music.

Before we started, and to warm up the crowd, a man from the resettlement office played the piano and sang "How Much is That Doggie in the Window?"

I don't know how Sammy knew to do this, but he barked two times after each line.

How much is that doggie in the window?

"Arf, arf!"

The one with the waggly tail?

"Arf, arf!"

The children in the audience smiled and laughed at his silliness. They didn't realize that he barked like that all the time.

Marilyn did a routine with Rocket to the "Theme from *Peter Gunn*." Marilyn wore a 1950s detective suit complete with fedora and had a huge magnifying glass. She began the routine by kneeling next to Rocket. She would hold her hand to her forehead like she was shielding her eyes from the sun. Both she and Rocket would first look to the right and then to the left before they broke out into their routine.

Our friend Meg danced with her Norfolk terrier, Pumpkin, to the "Theme from *Bonanza*." Both Meg and Pumpkin dressed as cowgirls with brown Stetsons.

The audience watched with rapt attention as our group danced with our dogs and then enthusiastically applauded us. Afterward, we allowed the children to pet the dogs. The small dogs were the crowd's favorites, but a few of them were brave enough to pet the greyhound.

When I wasn't dancing with Sammy, I felt invisible. I think that's a common complaint from women over a certain age, and I was no exception as I was in my fifties. Society ignores older women. Older men with silver hair are deemed handsome and debonair. Women with gray hair and glasses are passed by in the store by salesmen who want to serve the more youthful-looking woman. Doing something difficult like performing in front of a group of people gave me self-esteem and self-confidence. Having a sidekick like Sammy helped.

Suffolk is a small town, and soon we were known throughout as the women who danced with their dogs. It came as no surprise to us when we were invited to participate in a night-time holiday parade in Suffolk. Elyse designed red t-shirts for us, and we all wore Santa hats. Elyse also made large windup keys from cardboard that she spray-painted gold. We wanted the dogs to look like they were big toys with those keys attached to their harnesses. We had light-up leashes for each dog in red, green, and white. During the parade, we had a little routine where we would pretend like we were winding up the dogs. Then the dogs would spin beside us and circle us. We performed this in front of the judges, and the result was a second-place trophy for Best Animal Act in the parade. Maybe we weren't so invisible after all. We were bested by a group of the most adorable miniature horses dressed in red and green blankets with their manes and tails braided. Tough competition.

Chapter 26

Things That Go Bump in the Night

We have many dog beds in our house. In our bedroom, we have one greyhound-sized dog bed and one whippet-sized dog bed we got when Sammy was just a puppy. Sammy curls up into that whippet-sized bed every night. But when he gets up in the middle of the night to go outside, PG moves from the bigger bed to the whippet-sized bed. Then this causes Sammy to sleep on the floor, not in any bed at all, and since he's not sleeping anyway, he whines at about 4:30 a.m. to make me get up and take them on a walk. Maybe he thinks that after we get back from the walk and PG is distracted, he can get back in his own little bed.

What is so appealing about that lumpy, small bed that makes it so coveted?

And why is it that Alan can get up four or five times during the night—he could even do cartwheels if he wanted and was able to—and my dogs wouldn't even move a muscle.

But if I crack a slit in an eyelid or slightly move my pinky finger under the blanket, the dogs are right by my side! Are you getting up? Are we going on our walk now? Is it time for breakfast?

One spring night, my dogs woke me from a deep sleep. I mindlessly dragged myself down the stairs to let them outside. Off they ran into the moonlit yard from the laundry room stoop. Usually, they would only be outside for ten to fifteen minutes, so I wouldn't go back upstairs. I would sit on the sofa with my eyes closed and wait until I heard them on the porch again.

When I knew they wanted back inside, I didn't turn on any lights. I just opened the door like I had done a thousand times, and they both ran past me up the stairs. I plodded along behind them like an automaton, got into bed, and pulled up the covers. Soon I was asleep again.

Ker-thump. Ker-thump. I slowly became conscious of a strange noise. I didn't know if I was dreaming it or if I was hearing something. *Ker-thump.* I stared into the darkness. Where was that sound coming from?

To investigate, I swung my feet out from under the covers and turned on the light beside my bed. PG, my brindle greyhound, was lying near the foot of the bed with her eyes intently focused on the top of the stairs. And there was Sammy.

Sammy was lying Sphinx-like, flinging a dead rabbit in the air between his front paws. *Ker-thump.* The rabbit would hit the floor. He would cock his head and look at it, as if to say, "Get up and run again!" When the rabbit didn't comply, he would toss it into the air again. *Ker-thump.* PG watched him with fascination, also waiting for the rabbit to come back to life.

"Ewww," was what immediately came to my mind. "Now what am I going to do?" and "Why didn't I look out the door before I let them in?" were thoughts that followed shortly thereafter.

Both dogs were so focused on the rabbit that I could slip past Sammy and go back downstairs into the kitchen for a garbage bag. Clad in a pink-flowered nightgown and bare feet, I was not dressed in the best attire to wrench a fresh kill away from a young hound, but there was no time to change clothes. I knelt on the top step. The rabbit was dead, but it wasn't bloody, so my carpet was safe for a while. I needed to get it away from him before that scenario changed. I turned the garbage bag inside out around my hand and waited patiently for the rabbit to go airborne. When Sammy flung him three feet up in the air, I snatched the dead rabbit from between his paws. Quickly, I inverted the garbage bag with the rabbit inside, trying not to touch it, even through the plastic. Both dogs danced around me like cherubs in an Italian Renaissance painting as I took the rabbit outside to the garbage can. Only when the lid came down were they convinced the rabbit was gone for good.

At the racetrack, no matter how fast they run or how hard they try, they never catch the rabbit. This time it didn't get away from them. After that, I always looked outside before letting the dogs back into the house.

That paid off for me the night that PG showed up holding an opossum dangling by the scruff of its neck from her mouth. The opossum's rat-like tail was curled in a spiral, and its paws looked like little hands. I opened the screen door a few inches before I saw the opossum and then quickly slammed it shut. PG stood on the stoop looking up at me and couldn't understand why I wouldn't let her in.

"Drop it!" I yelled through the screen door. PG just wagged her tail.

I was thankful at that point that I didn't have a doggie door. PG would have carried that furry lizard right inside.

I closed the inside wooden kitchen door and leaned against it for a few moments. I turned on the porch light and peeked out the window. She was still standing on the porch looking expectantly at the door.

Again, I yelled, "Drop it!"

This time she complied. She went a few feet into the grass and released the opossum from her grip. I was sure it was dead.

She returned to the porch and made a short yip. I opened the door only wide enough for her to squeeze through. I didn't want her to trick me by turning around, picking up the opossum again, and charging into the house like Sammy had done with the rabbit.

In the morning, I looked out the back door to find the opossum was gone. They really do "play possum."

Chapter 27

Long Goodbye

What is the hardest part of adopting a rescue greyhound? The day you have to say goodbye.

On top of the seizures that Sammy continued to have, he also began showing signs of intestinal bowel disorder. He lost weight and had diarrhea almost all the time.

Sammy was only seven years old when his intestinal tract failed, and my vet diagnosed him with Inflammatory Bowel Syndrome. I had gone through this before with Kit. And now, on top of his seizures, he had another serious illness. Greyhounds are skinny to begin with, and he lost weight. I tried all the diets: the Canine Nutrigenomics diet; the White Diet where I fed him only white foods like fish and potatoes; the Sun Dog Cat Moon Diet where I fed him meat, vegetables, and dried turmeric that I cooked daily in a Crock-Pot; and the Raw Food Diet where I fed him only raw meat and vegetables. I gave him steroids and probiotics. We weighed him every week and would track how much weight he gained or lost in ounces. If he gained two or three ounces, it was a victory.

He seemed to go in waves—he seemed happy and played with PG sometimes, and then other times he hung his head and panted. I could tell he felt miserable. It was a balancing act of stress and meds, but he continued to get sicker and sicker.

I hired a dog walker to come mid-day to take Sammy and PG for a short walk through the neighborhood. Otherwise, I would have been cleaning up his accidents every day. Susie had been recommended by my vet, and I was not disappointed in her. I always knew she had been at the house because she left a red lipstick kiss mark on Sammy's head.

We communicated back and forth by text, and if the dogs did something unusual, she would drop me a short text about it.

But I never could have imagined what happened next. She had been coming to the house every day for about six months. One Friday, Susie texted me that she had to go to the emergency room. I thought she had just fallen and twisted an ankle or maybe got a cut that needed stitches while she was chopping some vegetables for dinner. I didn't pry into the reason but told her not to worry about it. I left work and walked the dogs myself that day. On Monday, she texted again. She had been admitted to the hospital and wouldn't be able to walk the dogs all week. She didn't explain her hospital stay, and again I didn't want to ask.

I didn't hear from her for two weeks. I texted her to say, "Hope all is well with you and that you're recovering from your hospital stay. Sammy and PG really miss you."

I immediately received a text back. "There is no easy way to tell you this. This is Susie's daughter. My mother passed away last week. She had ovarian cancer, and none of us knew."

I was floored and didn't know what to say. I texted back, "I'm so sorry to hear this. I only knew her for a short time, but I thought your mother was a wonderful woman."

Soon after this, I got an email from the organizers of James River Greyhounds that they needed volunteers for the weekend conference of the International Veterinary Acupuncture Society in Richmond. They needed both healthy dogs and a couple of sick ones, if possible, for the vets to practice on. Greyhounds are famous for working with vets because they are so laid back. I hoped veterinary acupuncture would produce a healing response in Sammy. I had tried so many things with him—this would be a last-ditch effort. I volunteered for him to be the sick dog.

I drove him to the hotel where they were holding the conference. Of course, he barked when he got there. It wouldn't be Sammy without the barking. In the morning, we sat in on some of the lectures, and in the afternoon, Sammy and I were front and center. I sat in front of the audience of vets in a bright red shirt. It wasn't the case, but I felt like there was a spotlight on us.

The vet who was running the session asked me some questions about Sammy's health. I calmly explained how he had developed the IBD on top of his seizures and how I had tried everything, but he kept getting sicker.

Suddenly, I started to cry.

"I love this dog so much. I don't know what will happen to me if I lose him." Embarrassed by my outburst, I buried my face into the side of Sammy's neck as several of the vets in the audience came up and put their hands on my shoulder or rubbed my back. There were murmurs of "It will be all right" and "You're going to be okay." It didn't comfort me.

A couple of the vets volunteered to work on him. The vet who was running the session explained to them precisely where they should insert the needles. They stuck needles along his spine that made him look like a very underweight stegosaurus. I swear I could see sunlight shine through his stomach and legs.

After the conference, I took time off work and continued to take him for another six months to the closest acupuncture vet I could find. She was from Richmond, but one day a week she practiced in an office in Williamsburg. In a lighthearted spirit, she kept calling Sammy "Chunky Monkey."

I thought to myself, "I should bring PG with me sometime so you can really see what a chunky monkey looks like!"

Sammy seemed to get a little better. We discussed doing a fecal transplant where donor stool from a healthy dog would be inserted into Sammy's colon. I was willing to try.

One day in December, he had a normal, firm stool, and I was so excited. I took it in to the office with me to show to the vet.

"Look at this firm poop," I squealed. I opened the plastic bag so the vet and her assistant could see.

"Maybe we're turning a corner," the vet said. I was optimistic. I hugged Sammy close to my chest.

On the night before Christmas Eve, I woke around 4:00 a.m. to the sound of Sammy vomiting. That is one sound that will quickly make me jump out of bed. When I turned on the lights, I saw that he had thrown up only blood. Despite the small progress he had made, I knew in my heart it was time to let him go.

I drove on dark, quiet streets to the emergency vet clinic. I practiced in the car saying out loud, "I need to have my dog put down," so I wouldn't break into tears when I got to the receptionist desk. I was the only one at the clinic when I arrived. I broke into tears despite my practice.

When I took him back to the exam room, I was still crying.

"Do you need a few more minutes with him?" the vet tech asked me.

I thought to myself, "I need a lifetime with him. With him dancing and barking beside me. A few more minutes with him in pain won't do anything for either of us."

"No. I'm ready," I said.

Under harsh fluorescent lights, I sat on the floor and cradled his head in my arms as the vet gave him the shot. He looked up at me one last time and loved me with his eyes. No more barking. He went limp. His tongue dropped out of the side of his mouth onto my leg, and he was gone. I walked out of the clinic into the dark winter night.

I lived in Hampton, and my adult children lived in Richmond. We had plans to stay overnight at a dog-friendly La Quinta hotel in Richmond on Christmas Eve. Our tradition was to eat dinner at a restaurant on Christmas Eve and then open gifts. My kids knew I had put Sammy down that morning, but we still went through the motions. We opened presents and tried to have fun.

"I'm sorry about Sammy, "Jade said, and Eric echoed that sentiment.

"I don't want to talk about it. It will just make me cry," I said as I tried to hold back the tears by biting my lip and fanning my hands in front of my face.

On Christmas morning, I woke up and went down to the hotel lobby for some breakfast. I was watching one of the morning shows when a dog food commercial came on TV. It showed a dog aging from a puppy through its senior years. When the boy in the commercial, who had by then become a young man, had to help his old, gray-faced dog jump into the car, I just lost it. I sat in the hotel lobby and sobbed quietly into a napkin. I could feel my heart breaking.

I know people say, "It's only a dog." But the grief I felt at losing that dog was remarkable. I would reach for a leash to take him on a walk, and then realize he wasn't there. The house was so quiet without his constant barking. I always told people he was making a joyful noise, and now my joyful noise was silent.

Sammy was my canine freestyle partner, so I thought listening to some music would help me. Over the next few days, I played some of our dancing songs, "Hit the Road, Jack", and "Puttin' on the Ritz." They made me smile. But playing the soundtrack from the Broadway show *Rent* was a mistake. The end of the song "I'll Cover You" brought me to my knees. How many times had Sammy covered me with kisses?

Even though I've since adopted several greyhounds, I never got over losing Sammy. He left a void in my heart that no other dog can fill.

Grief came in waves. When it first happened, I felt like I couldn't keep my head above the water. The height of the waves was over my head. I couldn't breathe. After a while, I would find some piece of him I could hold on to. I would see a photograph that would remind me. The Facebook memories could be gut punches. They would appear so randomly.

Sometimes they made me smile, and sometimes they made me cry. I waited for the waves to flatten out and roll gently onto the beach.

When Sammy passed, I lost my source of unconditional love. In some ways, he was like a child to me, and in other ways, he was my partner. Sammy couldn't stand to be away from me. If we went somewhere and I went into another room, even the restroom, he would bark and bark until I returned. It drove others crazy. I found it endearing. My relationship with Sammy was more satisfying than any of my human relationships. I cried more when Sammy died than when my parents died.

I took Sammy's ashes to Sandy Bottom Park where we walked hundreds of times, first with Radar and then with PG. On a cold winter morning, I scattered his ashes near the lake's edge at the spot where he used to jump in the water. No one told me that the ashes have little bone fragments in them and therefore are lighter in color than campfire ashes. I wasn't expecting that when I untwisted the metal tie from the plastic bag and began pouring them out. I tried to focus instead on the light over the lake and the sounds of the birds in the trees. Sammy would be in his "happy place," and I could release some of my grief every time I visited him there. Each time I walked by, there was less of a trace of the chalky white bits on the dirt. Eventually, it was completely unnoticeable, and Sammy was gone again.

Instead of saying "I miss you," my French friends say, "Tu me manques," which translates to "You are missing from me."

Sammy, tu me manques.

Chapter 28

Epilogue

It took me a year after losing Sammy, but I finally adopted another greyhound. I thought for a while that I would get a saluki. I remembered all the handwringing I had done on my French trip trying to decide on a breed of dog. I contacted the Sight Hound Underground Group in Washington, DC and asked about their available dogs. They rescue sighthounds from around the world and had access to galgos, podencos, and salukis, as well as greyhounds. I read a lot of information about salukis and discovered they can be fence jumpers. According to the adoption group, I would need at least a six-foot-tall privacy fence in my back yard, and I only had a four-foot-tall chain-link one. But they did have a couple of greyhounds that I could have if I was interested.

So I drove to DC on a Black Friday after Thanksgiving to meet Coheed. He is a black tuxedo male greyhound that was named after the rock group Coheed and Cambria. He came from a litter in Kansas where all the dogs were named after rock-and-roll groups. I kept the Coheed part of his name. If one has ever seen Coheed and Cambria, one might question why I kept that part of the name. Coheed, the rocker, is about seven feet tall with a head of wild dark hair like Rubeus Hagrid in *Harry Potter*. A slim, sleek greyhound looks nothing like that. One of my friends calls him Cochise—because she can never remember Coheed. And when someone on the street asks me what his name is, and they don't hear my answer correctly, they call him Cody as they scratch his head. I don't correct them.

Coheed will probably be my last dog for several reasons. For one, I'm getting older, and I can't lift him.

After our evening walks it became customary for Coheed to get a cup of doggie ice cream. On one such evening, Alan was holding the cup for him to lick, and he said, "There's blood all over the floor." Smears of blood trailed from the front door, through our foyer, and up the steps to the living-room chair where Alan was sitting. On our walk, Coheed had never yelped or lifted his foot. I didn't realize that anything was wrong.

When I knelt to check his pads and toes, I really couldn't see where the blood was coming from, but it was from some cut on his back foot. I wrapped the foot in gauze bandages and vet wrap and took him to the emergency vet. He was able to jump in the back of the car with his foot wrapped. But if he hadn't been able to jump up, I don't know what I would have done.

This happened during the Covid pandemic, and the policy at the emergency vet clinic was that the owner sat in the car while the animal was being treated.

I took him to the clinic at 7:00 p.m. Although I had wrapped his foot in vet wrap, he was leaving bloody footprints in the lobby of the clinic. One of the vet techs took him to the back examining area and placed him in a crate. She then asked me to return to my car.

At 11:00 p.m., the vet finally called me as I sat outside in the desolate parking lot. "Look, we are really backed up here. I'm probably not even going to look at his foot until three or four in the morning, and I don't want to take off the bandage that you put on it until I can treat him because the bleeding has finally stopped. Why don't you go home and get some sleep and come back here at 6:00 a.m. when we reopen the lobby?"

I reluctantly agreed. When I returned at six, she brought out a loopy Coheed with a huge plastic cone around his head.

"His right pinky toe on his back foot was almost completely severed. It was just hanging from a piece of skin. I removed it at the first knuckle, similar to what we do when we de-claw a cat. The outside toes aren't weight-bearing. He'll be fine when it heals. Take him to your vet in fourteen days and have her remove the three stitches I put in," the vet told me.

"I can't believe I didn't realize he did this. Thinking about it now, I think he was lifting his leg to pee on a tree, but the tree had one of those thick metal grates around it. When he shifted his weight to put his leg back down, the toe of the foot on the grate probably slipped down into one of the holes and got lopped off," I said.

The vet just grimaced.

Luckily, Alan came along with me to take Coheed home. He was so disoriented from the sedative that he couldn't jump into the back cargo area of the car. Alan was able to pick him up and place him in the cargo area. I wouldn't have been able to do that.

Another reason that Coheed may be my last dog is that I live in a condo now with no yard or other green space. I must leash walk Coheed. I cringe when it is pouring rain or snowing, and I know I must walk him on the slippery sidewalks. When I got sick myself with Covid, he had to go and stay with my daughter because I was unable to walk him. I realize I have limitations now when it comes to a large-breed dog.

But you know, at some point, someone from one of the adoption groups may call me and say, "Joyce, can you go and pick up this hound?" And given my track record, I'll be right back in it.

Acknowledgements

Writing a book about one's life is harder than I thought. I'm forever indebted to the following people who helped bring my story to fruition.

Thank you to Marilyn Sanders for reading my first rough draft, for correcting all my errors pertaining to dog training and for giving me suggestions on changes.

Thank you to Jennie Harris, Marilyn Paolino, and Kirsten Tartano for reading the manuscript and being honest about needed revisions.

Thank you to Lesley St. James for being a thorough, attentive editor.

Thank you to Lisa Thomas for the quirky cover art and to Oliver Dimalanta for pulling the whole book cover together.

Thank you to Sarah Kane Photography for the amazing author photo on the back cover.

And finally thank you to my husband Alan Gavalya for being my biggest cheerleader and always supporting me.
I couldn't have done it without your help.

ABOUT THE AUTHOR

Joyce and Kit photographed by Alan R. Gavalya

Joyce and Sammy photographed by Alan R. Gavalya

Joyce A. Miller adopted six greyhounds over the past twenty years and danced with several of them. Miller lives in the Church Hill section of Richmond, Virginia, with her husband and her latest retired racing greyhound. Before she started writing, Miller worked for over thirty years as a mechanical designer at a nuclear physics laboratory. When she is not writing, Miller can be found dog training, painting, practicing yoga, traveling with her French physicist friends, tap dancing, or volunteering with her greyhound adoption group.

Connect with Miller online at www.joyceamiller.com where you can learn more about her.

www.ingramcontent.com/pod-product-compliance
Lightning Source LLC
Chambersburg PA
CBHW012208090526
44583CB00023BA/2967